Let's Walk, Lilly

Lilly and Russ   painting by Jo Chinard

Let's Walk, Lilly

AN ARMCHAIR COMPANION
TO
TRAILS ON

MARTHA'S VINEYARD

by
Russell Hoxsie

The articles in this collection appeared previously in
The Martha's Vineyard Times.

For information about permission to reproduce selections

from this book, write MV Times Press

PO Box 518

Vineyard Haven, MA 02568

visit us at mvtimes.com

ISBN 0-9760401-0-7 (HC)

ISBN 0-9760401-1-5 (PB)

Library of Congress Control Number: 2004111563

Printed in the United States of America

Book design by Tony Omer

*Dedicated to
Mary Ann*

Acknowledgments

I want to thank Niki Patton, fellow writing group member and frequent contributor to The Martha's Vineyard Times, for first suggesting this inexperienced writer to the Calendar editor of The Times as a possible contributor for a series of "walks" articles. She, like Nancy Aronie at the Chilmark Writing Workshop, was a source of encouragement in my writing what is not only in the head but more importantly what is from the heart. Perry Garfinkel as editor saw me through my first uneven days when I was not used to meeting deadlines and needed the often unheeded suggestion that I get my pieces filed ahead of time – good discipline for a procrastinator. He gave me my first encouragement as a fledgling columnist. Likewise Pat Waring, current editor has been unstinting in praise and encouragement, even suggesting I return to my routine after many months of absence following illness. She gave me back some good reason to be around instead of vegetating. Will Flender's little spiral "Walking Trails of Martha's Vineyard" (first and second editions) was invaluable in finding places I hadn't dreamed were there, figuring mileage from place to place and knowing some of the features to look for ahead of time. He treated me to the private Meetinghouse Association Trail and we helped pick ticks off each other and my springer friend, Lilly, after a walk there. The Land Bank's "Public Conservation Lands Map" was a frequent and valued reference and guide as was Ted Thomas's "Martha's Vineyard Detailed Road Map." As a freelancer at The Times, I often encountered faces there I did not recognize, but entering that large press room off Beach Road always left a warm feeling of welcome, despite its being the nerve center of a busy newspaper. Anna Marie D'Addarie, associate Calendar editor, has continued the great reception I've felt at the paper with my new project "Off North Road." I have been blown away by the quality of the photographs and sketches which accompany each article in "Lilly." Many of them are new and enhance the work immeasurably. I am very grateful to Kenneth Vincent for his sure-handed and stark sketches that capture the locales he visited. Ralph Stewart contributed many fine photos including one of the author in a tentative pose atop Waskosim's Rock; Susan Safford, Sara Piazza, Tyson Trish, Tim Johnson, Mae Deary, Stephen Warriner, Bob Schellhammer, Betsy Corsiglia and Julian K. Robinson all contributed handsomely. I am honored to appear in their company. Many others of The Times's crew have at one time or another had a hand in helping with my columns: Tori Socha, Amy Simcik Williams, Mae Deary, Dan Cabot I remember. I thank them for proofing and performing other chores I am clearly unaware of. Tony Omer has dealt with the final form of the book, now reduced to a single CD before publication. He seems always to be able to answer my questions about computers and what to do about this and that. He is responsible for the book's coming to life. Thanks to everyone. Doug Cabral, Editor and chief honcho, was always excited about this project, even with delays and my plaintive inquiries of, "How long will it take?" Peter Oberfest, Publisher and Christmas party host with Barbara, essentially reinforced everyone's contribution by his own enthusiasm. I especially thank my old friend, Jo Chinard, who took up painting at the tender age of sixty, for her painting of the old man and his dog and approving its use on the cover. My wife Mary Ann heard me read every article one or several times and helped me avoid some egregious errors. Of course it goes without saying I will always remember Lilly as my faithful walking companion.

Table of Contents

The name of the walk is followed by its location,
owner, and page number. Directions to the beginning of each
walk follows the essay.

INTRODUCTION

Sometime in the summer of 1999, Perry Garfinkel, then editor of the Calendar section of The Martha's Vineyard Times, called out of the blue and asked me to tell him my favorite Vineyard walk. I was taken completely by surprise; the question from this stranger had seemed odd at the time. After a long hesitation, I said "Well, I guess I have to say Flanders Lane in Chilmark." To be truthful, I could think of none other at the moment. I walk there several times a week and, if not my favorite, it is at least the most familiar. Perry said he had the idea of a regular Walks column for the paper and Niki Patton, fellow member of my writer's group and frequent contributor to The Times, had recommended me as a candidate for implementing his idea. With no previous experience at writing regularly for a newspaper or anyone else, I said I would try it and if he liked what I wrote he might ask me to continue. This was the beginning then of nearly three years of writing my semi-monthly columns. My first reaction was to think that I never wanted to live by any more deadlines after my long life in the arduous practice of medicine. My second reaction after about three months was of embarrassment that I was seeing places on my island home of 45 years for the first time. "I didn't know this place was here!" became a sort of mantra. Although I never grew really accustomed to a deadline (my pieces began arriving later and later), I began to feel I was accumulating experiences I should have had years before and actually loved hearing the occasional word on the street that someone felt she was actually walking the walk as she read about it. I began using my dictionary and spell-check often, realizing I was not the great speller I had thought. I learned to take a water bottle along in warm weather not only for me but for my wonderful companion, Lilly, my springer spaniel, who walked and rummaged with me for most of my excursions. I learned more Vineyard history, especially some of the early happenings to the first Vineyarders, the Native Americans. I read about processing wool and what the term fulling means (the shrinking and thickening of cloth, especially wool, by exposure to moisture and pressure). I made several good friends by asking them to walk with me and explain what they did for a living or what interested them the most about the Vineyard. Above all, I renewed my great love for the outdoors, the exhilaration of exercising and its after-effect of feeling comfortably achy and tired enough for a good nap on return home. I learned humility by making mistakes in the public realm of a newspaper article. Some were small like misspelling Wilfrid's Pond at Tashmoo in Tisbury and some were monumental like forgetting that current theory pretty well proves the great mountain ranges were not the result of gouging out and raising up great gobs of primitive earth by advancing glaciers (as our own humble moraines were raised up) but that tectonic plates well beneath the earth's surface, shift and collide with each other resulting in buckling upward of the great mountain ranges. Fortunately all of those bringing attention to these gaffs were kindly disposed and set me straight with minimum embarrassment. I remain grateful to them. Incidentally, as time went on, I became more careful in my scholarship. What some may feel is missing from this work is more description of Martha's Vineyard as a whole. I would urge those interested to pursue some of the sources I mention: Walking in Vineyard Haven by James H. K. Norton, Moraine to Marsh by Ann Hale, Redman's Land / White Man's Law by W.E. Washburn, The Patriot Chief by A.M. Josephy, The Invasion of North America by Francis Jennings, and History of Martha's Vineyard by Charles M. Banks. Other sources abound in the different towns' public libraries and the Martha's Vineyard Historical Society's publication, The Intelligencer. Whatever your interests, whether they be in a comfortable chair by a warm stove or fireplace, in occasional excursions into one or two of the many Vineyard trails, or in making a habit of them as I have, you will be guaranteed pleasure, exercise, and a story or two to tell about that wonderful island we know as Martha's Vineyard.

Imagine, if you can, you're in a time machine back 10,000 years .... "Well, that's the way my first account in the Winter section begins as I set out to enjoy another walking trail on Martha's Vineyard. This is not a science-fiction book or even a travel book. It's a casual approach to the fascinating environment of the Vineyard and an illustration of having fun year-round while enjoying and exploring some walking trails. They're available to anyone with reasonably sound legs and an excuse to go out in the fresh air. You and I will walk in these pages over the terminal moraine left by the last advance of a glacier ten thousand years ago. We will pass from the busy summer streets of town into the serenity of Sheriff's Meadow Preserve right in the center of Edgartown. We'll climb the winding hills in Chilmark to look down the Mill River Valley toward Tisbury from Waskosim's Rock and we'll listen for the sharp crack of a deer's foot on a twig at Menemsha Hills on the way to the great overlook sand cliff on Vineyard Sound.

You may want to travel alone and enjoy the quiet or the wind or watch the sun come up over North Neck one cold morning on Chappaquiddick. I've often taken my springer, Lilly, and shuffled through the falling leaves anywhere autumn skies beckon. Or, and this is the most fun for many, you can join a guided walk with a naturalist from The Trustees of Reservations or the Martha's Land Bank and learn more about flora and fauna at Wasque or preserving sand plains at Long Point.

INTRODUCTION

This is a book to dip in and out of as the spirit moves. Simple directions for finding each trail occupy an appendix in the same order as the walks are presented. The walks are arranged by season as an encouragement, for everybody who can, to go all over the island whatever the temperature or weather. For those who cannot walk the trails, I hope these glimpses into some of our hidden treasures will bring you there in mind and spirit. Historical references will be found for those interested in how some things came to be here. Native and AfricanAmericans have played a significant role in Vineyard development. You will be able to follow the African-American Heritage Trail and visit Aquinnah (Gay Head) for a personal experience in the diversity of Martha's Vineyard.

When you think you have discovered all the trails and all the interesting places to visit, think again. Once you've whetted your appetite, you'll probably find many more, enough to keep you satisfied for a life time. Walk in health!

Russ Hoxsie
Chilmark, July 2004

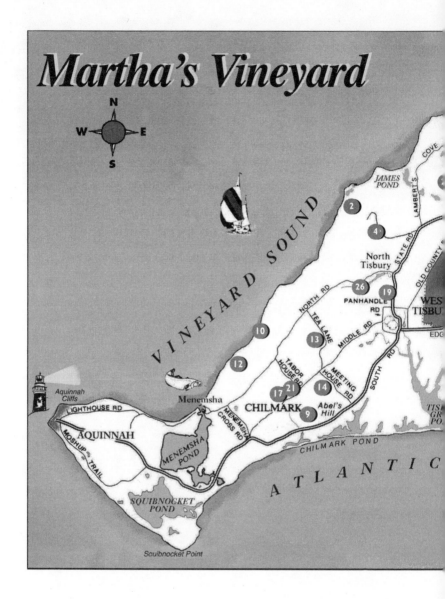

Martha's Vineyard

N
W · E
S

VINEYARD SOUND

JAMES
POND

LAMBERT'S COVE

2

4

North
Tisbury

STATE RD.

OLD COUNTY RD.

26

19

WES
TISBU

PANHANDLE
RD.

NORTH RD.

TEA LANE

MIDDLE RD.

EDG

10

13

SOUTH RD.

12

TABOR HOUSE RD.

MEETING HOUSE RD.

17 21

14

Menemsha

CHILMARK

9

Abel's
Hill

TIS
GR
PO.

Aquinnah
Cliffs

LIGHTHOUSE RD.

MENEMSHA CROSS RD.

CHILMARK POND

AQUINNAH

MOSHUP TRAIL

MENEMSHA
POND

ATLANTIC

SQUIBNOCKET
POND

Squibnocket Point

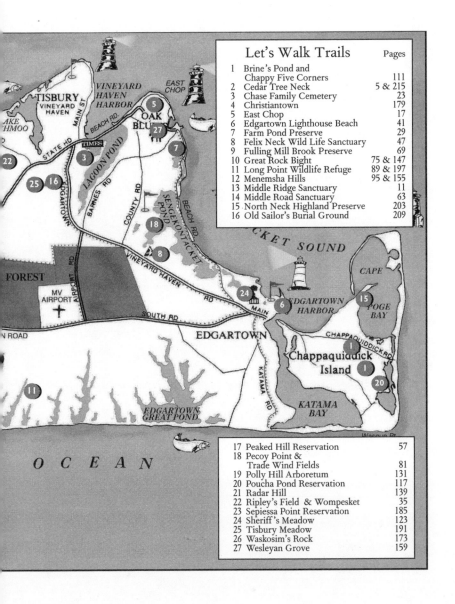

SPRING

A retired octogenarian once confided to me over the back fence that she hated the wind on Martha's Vineyard. However, she stuck it out until the natural order of things relieved her for all time. I sympathized with her and will stick it out also. Our friends "in America" think of March as the month with gale winds but their saving grace is sharing those lions with a lamb at the beginning or end. Here on the Vineyard that god of legend whose pursed lips carry winds far and wide comes in with a vengeance sometime in the fall and stays around for several days at a time until summer. Springtime comes to us haltingly and late. The forsythia blooms along Boston's Commonwealth Avenue weeks before ours dare to show. Walking anywhere becomes unpredictable underfoot. Trails in the lowlands run with little streams or the woods suddenly develop a marsh of several acres. Nights are penetrated by the steady howl of Neptune's testy breath and my old friend's exasperation with him rings in my ears. Part of Vineyard life dictates we survive this wet, rainy, wind- blown season.

Now we look forward impatiently to warm breezes, hot sand and cool water for swimming. Fishermen have repaired their gear and are champing for a good day on the beach or bay. Yet the months of March and April hang to the cold and May, though sunny, may be no better. Even in June the air retains a chill and swims are quick in-and-outs. Despite all this, the peak season awaits and we're glad. For that walk at Long Point, waterproof footwear serves well but even then you may have to detour around the flooded banks of Tiah's Cove. The newly sprung marsh on both sides of the path to Menemsha Pond may precipitate a sudden sitz-bath in mud and a good laugh at how soft your landing feels. No matter the warmth of the sun at your back door, wear sweatshirt and gloves and you'll be comfortable near the ocean. Don't forget the ticks which begin to seek blood when you least expect them. Tuck your pants inside your socks and look decidedly uncool. After all you're in the woods on the Vineyard!

Springtime is the season of renewal; a glimpse of mayflowers protruding up from under old leaves is a fitting reward for the wet bum. You may see a snapping turtle lumbering up from her swampy home near the pond to lay eggs and hope her progeny will survive to return. Beware her snapping jaws on protruding neck. Gus Ben David at Felix Neck calls her the most dangerous wild animal here. Southern birds are flying in and the first osprey sighted on a familiar nesting pole deserves mention in the news. Kids won't mind the cold ocean at Memorial Day. It's the time I always raced from school to have my first plunge although a few unbalanced folk tried Patriot's Day in April to make the pilgrimage.

The wild pear's delicate bloom is among the first to break the gray-black bleakness of the woods and later the whole panorama of wood-tops down the long Mill Valley from Waskosim's Rock to Vineyard Haven take on the faintest pink glaze before turning through shades of green to the finished oak canopy. Tiasquam River gurgles with the briskness of spring flood and, as the thermometer tentatively climbs, the freshly hatched cygnets on inland ponds begin to caravan through shore-line reeds in their kindergarten explorations. Land and waters have conquered the cold and finally burst into new-found life again, the greatest teachers of Vineyard patience there is.

Ralph Stewart

Cedar Tree Neck

Susan Safford

Cedar Tree Neck

It's the last week in March and the lamb is trying to outlast the lion, temperature in the fifties and wind light although gusty on the beach. Lilly and I are off to walk the trails at Cedar Tree Neck, the 216 acre sanctuary maintained by Sheriff's Meadow Foundation. The old dirt road is considerably improved since the last time I was here twenty-five years ago. Well placed "Sanctuary" signs lead us to the parking lot a mile at the end. The sun outside the car is unseasonably warm and I doff my sweater and tuck my pant legs into my socks. The deer ticks are out aplenty the past week. We've been picking them off Lilly and "storing" them in strong soap solution on the kitchen counter. No Lyme Disease again for me this year.

Along with maps and trail guides and history of the sanctuary, someone has posted lovely colored photos of a scarlet tanager, oven bird, veery, red-eyed vireo and wood thrush. Only one is on my life-time list. Possibly you'll see one of these if you are sharp-eyed is the implication. The caveat, of course, is that they are rarely seen in the day-time and unlikely on such an early day in March. The pictures spur me on. The White Trail leads up from the southeast corner of the parking lot and within moments I see a nuthatch, common with his upside-down-walking on tree trunks but good enough. It's the last bird I'll see today except for gulls later at the beach. Still, no vireo.

The stillness of the bare oak woods now entered is relaxing. The breeze is all but muted here. At the top of the first hill (it is a hilly course altogether I'll find) is a grove of tall straight pines, something I see rarely on the Vineyard except where planted by man. It has yet to be replaced by the ubiquitous oak. I lead Lilly, who is sniffing at every tree trunk and under every pile of moist leaves, to the right fork of the Bruce Irons Trail. Before we have gone five minutes I am sitting on a bench looking over the stillness of Ames Pond. A flash of a bird disappears to my right before recognition. Everything else is suspended. The only ripple in the water is near Lilly's feet as she laps up some of the cold clear pond. Later in the season we would see turtles, perhaps, water bugs, and whirligig beetles and hear peepers, excuse me, pinkletinks. The weather is too cold today for these creatures although I've heard reports of the latter from those with better hearing than mine. The sound of pinkletinks is a sure sign of Spring.

We move down and then up to a beech grove, enormous gray trunked trees with gnarled roots stretching out in all directions, making footing a little treacherous. They have the knack of crowding out all other species of trees. We are following the course of the stream from Ames Pond. Later it joins another to form a common route to the sound beyond the dunes. At the top of a hill is a magical grove of pigmy beeches, stunted by the fierce winds of winter into brutish shapes reminding me of medieval dwarfs from old fairy tales. Their huge trunks and horizontal branches are forced back from skyward, their strength channeled toward earth and stillness.

Soon we descend to the beach and rocky north shore, scanning in a glance from Cutty Hunk to Woods Hole and beyond. The glitter on the sea this afternoon is beyond dazzling. A black dog in the distance clambers over the bushes into a small pond behind the dunes.

The Brown Trail leads off the beach to the north and takes a loop around the headland, on one side the edge of a fresh pond. I look down ten feet to the water below, clear, unruffled, with a few tiny trails leading to water for muskrats, deer, and, when the drop is less precipitous, for Lilly. On the upper limb of the trail is another view of the sound and the islands. A bench allows a few minutes of relaxation and marveling at the excitement engendered in repeated views of the same scenery from different perspectives.

The second time along the beach back to the trail toward home tells me I've walked a bit today. The sand is loose and each step takes more energy than I have remaining. I decide to put off the dramatically inclined long White Trail through the Alex Reed Bird Sanctuary for another day. Soon we're back into the woods along another ridge with ocean view. My red truck glistens through the trees to tell us we're finished.

As a young boy, I often put myself back into the "old days", days long gone but somehow known about by stories probably from father or grandfathers. What would it be like to be back in those ancient times? I think about this today when I pass through the woods, especially on the way down Obed Daggett Road and see stonewalls coursing every which-way through the woods. Those woods must have been pastures for cows and sheep, I think. And that old house near the water, the old Daggett Place, I imagine. People lived here a hundred, two hundred years, ago. Before electricity, trucks, mechanized farm machinery - isolated by distance from Vineyard towns. I imagine Obed Daggett gong out to mend his stone walls and tend his animals, looking for the spring lamb lost on a rocky hillside. I wonder how far he could see across the hilly pastures without the growth of forest we see now. I wonder how he got his milk or sheep to market. Did he butcher them himself? How long did the milk last without souring in a cold crock down under the cellar stairs?

I bought a package of corn bread mix at Cronig's today to stir up for supper. What did Mrs. Daggett do about corn bread? Had she to grind the corn, evaporate the salt, go to town for sugar and other flour? Her own chickens most likely provided the eggs. Did she cook corn bread in a wood stove oven or in a skillet over coal? I think I've done quite a good walk today, a little over an hour. Old Mr. Daggett probably walked up and down this moraine each day of his life just getting around the place.

I've read some of Ann Hale's "Moraine to Marsh" this week. She captures the feeling of Cedar Tree Neck, its geology, flora and fauna and much more. Today I've seen this special place she described so well and some of its people have crept into the mind's eye of a boy.

HOW TO GET THERE: Heading from Vineyard Haven, we veer off State Road to the right, just above the upper limb of Lambert's Cove Road in West Tisbury, onto Christiantown Road. We go 1.7 miles and turn to the right on Obed Daggett Road.

SPRING

Middle Ridge   Ralph Stewart

Climbing Middle Ridge
in Search of Spring

The day of our planned walk on Middle Ridge Preserve begins with dense fog and threat of rain. We can't see Menemsha Pond from our windows and it seems best to cancel plans, but the forecast is for sunshine by mid-morning. Lilly, our springer, and I decided to finish some small chores about the house and wait. My second cup of coffee is accompanied by a dozen crows circling and building a commotion to the northwest just beyond the marsh, and the sun begins to show through in thin streams before ten o'clock. We're off to Middle Road to see something new.

Middle Ridge is a seven-acre preserve acquired by the Martha's Vineyard Land Bank Commission in 1994. It sits atop the middle one of three ridges that run the length of Martha's Vineyard east to west (or, in common parlance, up and down-Island). We drive up Tea Lane from Middle Road and turn in at the land bank logo on the right side to park the pick-up. Fresh deer tracks greet us as we hop down to the sand in the parking lot. By now the fog is dispersed and the sun is bright enough for the long distance view of the south side I've been told about. The pine and oak woods we enter on a rather steep path uphill is soft underfoot. Spring has begun only barely at this high point. The blacks and grays and wet browns give way here and there to thin green strands of bull briars arching everywhere among low bush. Some even attain a height above me on their way to taller trees.

LET'S WALK, LILLY

Too soon for a needed rest we come to a bench. We've only just begun our hike and Lilly is impatient to keep moving, but the view to the south is arresting and I sit for a few moments to drink in the distance over bare tree limbs not yet pink with buds. Tisbury Great Pond lies behind the curving shoreline with its thin barrier dunes. The view sends me back in time 65 years to my uncle's barn in Barre, where I often snuck away from my chores and ascended the cupola through the dark, musty hay mows to watch out over the central Massachusetts hills to the valley and Wachusett Mountain in the distance. It always gave me a thrill and the realization that I could get away from the world simply by climbing to that place by myself before Uncle Wallace called me down for fear I'd break my neck. This ridge must have tickled some old connections to take me back there this morning.

We continue on toward the west on a well marked trail. Another vista gives us a look back to the north and the next ridge forming the complicated spine of the Vineyard. The trail descends at a rather steep pitch into more dense woods. Bikers and horses are excluded from this part of the loop because of the steep slope. I can see now that the oaks are fattening their buds and the beetlebungs, looking almost dead, sure enough have tiny buds forming to belie my first impression. It seems to me that the lower we descend, the fatter the buds become. Signs of habitation appear along the way, a cleared field and an enormous reserve of rocks and boulders, some eight feet high, resting at one end. An old rusted accumulation of housewares and other junk lurks in the distance on private property, signs of a hundred year old preserve for the really adventurous soul to begin digging over. I remember the terrible poison ivy my wife and her friend contracted on their last such foray many years ago.

I'm privileged this day to see far into the woods and out of the woods before the leaves burst and hide the view I have today. The trail ends at Middle Road at a spot I've traveled many times without taking notice of. A short walk to the right brings us to the bottom of Tea Lane. Lilly is panting and needs water. We share the same bottle and I pick the first small deer ticks of the season from her front legs. Lyme disease season, alas, is coming. We walk along Tea Lane a half mile, crossing two or three small streamlets gurgling under the road, coursing their way to Middle Road and beyond as they help form the river called Tiasquam on its way to the sea at Town Cove in West Tisbury. We return to the trail head and our truck. Lilly has begun to lag on the way, and she's content to collapse on the front seat after another drink. We've walked a mile and a half, not far, but a considerable portion of the distance was uphill. I'm glad to sit, too.

On our way back up Tea Lane toward North Road, we turn to the right just beyond the Middle Ridge parking lot onto Old Farm Road. This will be one of the connections the land bank hopes to make in the future with Waskosim's Rock Reservation off North Road. We see several tastefully built and arranged homes along this newly developed way. After a sharp turn to the north we pass the trail connection for walkers to the Waskosim's reservation and then arrive at North Road. For more ambitious walkers than I am this morning, the walk around Middle Ridge Preserve, thence to Old Farm Road and Waskosim's Reservation and back, would be an enjoyable good day's work. We've waited out the weather, to our great satisfaction, and have seen another preserve that takes us out of the world of bustle. After this promising beginning, I'll come back when spring is in full flower.

HOW TO GET THERE: : Drive to Tea Lane on Middle Road in Chilmark, then 0.6 mi. on Tea Lane to the Land Bank logo on the down-island side to the trail head and parking. A short quarter mile hike takes you around the trail loop with spectacular views from its high point. A longer trail branches from the loop across a private right-of-way to Middle Rd. Bikers and horses are excluded because of the steep slope. A short walk up Middle Rd. brings you to Tea Lane and the trail head. For a much longer walk, you can continue up Tea Lane to Old Farm Road and walk to the trail connection, well marked, for Waskosim's Rock Reservation. There is no parking along Old Farm Road or at the Waskosim's trail connection. Driving, you can go all the way to North Road, turn down-island and find the Waskosim's trail head and parking plainly marked a short distance on the right going toward West Tisbury.

SPRING

East Chop Light

Sara Piazza

East Chop

Jonathan Grout, Jr. hurries eagerly along the spit of beach toward East Chop on a clear morning in 1828 hoping that his newly erected "telegraph" signal tower on the bluff will expedite news-gathering from long-absent freight vessels and whalers as they make first landfall. He climbs the ladder to his platform pointed toward Muskeget and Nantucket, catching his breath as he makes out through his spy glass distant movement of signals on the horizon. The "Mercury" has made port at Nantucket bearing "treasures" from Sumatra. With great energy he begins transmitting the news to Woods Hole by raising and lowering huge arms and flags in semaphore fashion. From there his words are relayed to Bonnedale [?Bournedale], South Plymouth, Marshfield, and Dorchester Heights. It is hard to believe that signals visible from one set of eyes to another can be transmitted in this fashion but so they must have been on Telegraph Hill, nine years before Samuel F. B. Morse demonstrates his telegraphy and 14 years before he invents Morse Code. The East Chop Light rises on the site of one of the first telegraph signals. The "Mercury" is the first such ship to be reported this way. Alas, Mr. Grout's innovation lasts here only six years.

How many times have I driven along Beach Road to Oak Bluffs and neglected to turn on East Chop Drive, denying myself the pleasure of viewing the light house and old-century summer "cottages" along the bluff? Lilly, my springer, and I turn in and park on the shoulder at the curve, setting out along Grout's first telegraph walk. I'm thinking it must take courage (or is it foolhardiness?) to perch these attractive cottages at the edge of a narrow pebbly beach where the waves lap up only a few feet from the inevitable porch facing the water. And it takes ingenuity to provide the mundane but essential septic system this close to the water. Neither factor detracts from the joy in summer of such proximity to a pre-breakfast swim or the sound and smells of the salt water and fresh air. I am mistaken that this joy comes only in summer when I realize at least two of the cottages are occupied year-round. In the distance the ferry Islander heads to port as a freight boat crosses its bow toward Woods Hole. A few buffle heads swim quietly away as Lilly and I approach. The shore looks out upon Vineyard Haven harbor and West Chop across the bay. Farther to the north is Woods Hole, Cape Cod stretching out of view to the east. Today the sky holds overcast, the sea leaden. On other days with a bright sky the water is purest blue and in stormy weather one feels a little threatened by the spray cascading up the beach and the white caps which seem to roll all the way from West Chop. We pass a mocking bird in among the branches of a smartly trimmed holly. He seems to be asking why we are walking along here on a quiet morning. I stop to examine him, barely five feet away, and in a flash he disappears into the bush's depth. On the "land-side" of the road, a diminutive house nestles down, looking more like a doll house than a home for humans. When I first saw this place I thought only tiny people could live there until I met the owner, an elderly woman, tall and regal.

We climb a steep grade to the base of the lighthouse standing on the bluff looking to Nantucket Sound. Until 1988 when it was painted white, it was called the chocolate lighthouse because of its reddish-brown paint. Today it glistens against the sky. In the mid-1800's, Silas Daggett built the first privately operated light here, funded by local merchants who sailed in the area and by ships passing through. However, many of the ships, once safely anchored, refused to pay. The light ceased operation after only six years. By 1875, the U.S. government bought the land and erected the first cast-iron structure, 79 feet above the sea. Today the light is maintained and operated by the Martha's Vineyard Historical Society.

We are now in full view of the waters surrounding the chop, Vineyard Sound to the left and Nantucket Sound straight ahead. The long bony finger of Cape Pogue points toward the shoals of Cape Cod as if in warning to unwary sailors. Muskeget and Nantucket are beyond to the southeast out of site from our vantage. Along the steep bluff a row of summer "cottages", their lawns barely thirty feet from the edge, stand tall and angular, some more spread out than vertical. Nearly all have compound roofs with many gables. There are pitched dormers and shed dormers - single, double and quadruple - hips of varying pitch and angles; all have wrap-around porches of different shapes and sizes. Towers rise on several, some square, a few conical, one a nearly perfect upside-down ice cream cone. Here and there, wheat colored shingles bespeak of repairs and new construction. An occasional new modern dwelling peeks out with some embarrassment from behind its staid Victorian neighbors.

East Chop Drive descends gradually ahead toward a curve around Oak Bluffs harbor; we take a right on Brewster Avenue for a look behind the row of grand houses. Here we find many smaller summer cottages reminiscent of the Wesleyan Grove campground, all with porches facing the street and many with small second story galleries outside the front bedroom. The streets are a tangle of tarred and dirt roads. Someone said the designer of the original Cottage City never saw a straight line he liked. His philosophy certainly reigns here. Although mostly a summer colony, more and more of the neighborhood appears to be year-round as we approach New York Avenue via Munroe. The presence of five tennis courts attests to the interest of a good number of the residents.

It's time for a little rest and the Community Solar Greenhouse off New York Avenue offers the needed break. Toni Neil, Jane Brown and Chuck McBride are working away in an atmosphere one must describe as tropical. It is enough to fog eye glasses and force a visitor to reach for the zipper of a winter jacket. Geranium, Diplodenia, petunias, lime-light, lettuce and mesclun, basil and three-foot-high tomato plants flourish in the heat and moisture. This out-of-the-way institution is one of the most overlooked on the Vineyard, providing hands-on contact with Mother Earth and growing-things during the long bleak winter days outside. Lilly now is panting and we head for the car down the road. "Don't forget our annual seedling sale in May," say Toni and Jane in one breath as we leave.

We keep to the side of New York Avenue as far from passing cars and truck as we can. Harking back to Telegraph Hill, I still marvel at the ingenuity of old Jonathan Grout's giant semaphores 75 years before Marconi made his first trans-Atlantic radio transmission.

I am indebted to Arthur Railton and James Norton, both Vineyard historians of note, for confirming that a line of telegraph (semaphore) stations existed in the early 1800's from Boston to the Vineyard; to Martha's Vineyard Chamber of Commerce for an article by the late Gerald Kelly, "Martha's Vineyard Lighthouses", on line at www.mvy.com/lighthouses.html; to James Freeman for "Dukes County 1804" in The Dukes County Intelligencer, May 1971, vol.12, No. 4; and to Britannica.com for information on Samuel F.B. Morse and Guglielmo Marconi

HOW TO GET THERE: From Vineyard Haven drive past the hospital entrance on Beach Road, turn left on Temahigan past the State Police Barracks. At the junction with New York Avenue (the sharp curve to the right after the barracks) turn carefully against traffic to the left onto East Chop Drive. Pull onto the wide shoulder at the first curve to park. Proceed along the water to the right. Once past the lighthouse and row of large "cottages", take Brewster Avenue on the right, turn left at Munroe to New York Avenue and return right to park. From Edgartown, go through Oak Bluffs and proceed along New York Avenue passing straight through the curve onto East Chop Drive.

Chase Cemetary   Sara Piazza

The Chase Family Cemetery in Eighteenth Century Homses Hole

I have wandered in fascination over many old cemeteries. The stark reality of running hands and fingers over worn grave stones or stepping around sunken hollows of collapsed coffins gives familiarity to the idea that people lived and breathed in another century, or two or three centuries removed. I find a visit to an ancient burial place a way of viewing death from a distance without tears and grief, simply with a nostalgia and curiosity about times past. Being able to place in context some of the lives of those buried in the oldest cemetery in Vineyard Haven, to conjure up the lives they may have lived - what they accomplished or failed at - is an extraordinary experience. For this particular visit, James H. K. Norton's beautiful and well researched book, "Walking in Vineyard Haven," enables me to do just that.

Ellen Reynolds, Activities Director at Up-Island Council on Aging (COA), invites me to walk with a group of seniors and find the oldest cemetery in Vineyard Haven. We join another group from Tisbury and set out on our first spring-like day in mid March. Sandy Whitworth of the Tisbury COA leads our ragged line of walkers down State Road, courageously stopping cars and trucks to allow our crossing the heavily trafficked highway. We ascend the incline of Delano Road to a gently sloping graveyard facing Vineyard Haven Harbor and the Lagoon through a line of trees and bushes poised high above Causeway Road below. "You must look for the oldest grave here," Sandy tells us. While the group disperses over the hillside, Sandy begins the tale of the dominance of the Chase family over the beginnings of the settlement of Homses Hole Harbor and eventually the village of Vineyard Haven.

By all accounts the early name of Homses Hole should have been Chasetown or Chaseville or, in the European mode, Chase-On-the-Sea. The origin of the original name is unknown and it was late in the 18th century before its spelling was changed in honor of John Holmes, a local pilot and chandler. Reading in the early pages of Jim Norton's book illustrates the influence of Isaac Chase from the time of his first appearance in 1674 on the Vineyard applying for residence at Newtown (North Tisbury). His rejection from that community may have been his pro-Quaker leanings, anathema to many strictly Puritan New Englanders of the time. Moving on to Homses Hole with his friend from England, Jacob Perkins, Isaac helped Perkins build a home on four acres of land bought from Governor Thomas Mayhew which ran from the harbor near the present five corners to the south of the cart track to Newtown (now Beach Road). Within two years Perkins moved away and deeded over his property to Isaac. This became the original Chase family home where Mary Chase gave birth to six sons and six daughters. When the last of those bearing the surname Chase had left Vineyard Haven in 1825, most of the land and buildings of the entire harbor settlement had been bought or developed by the extended family of Isaac. The presence of the family was carried on by several generations of daughters, most of them descendants of Isaac's oldest son, Thomas, who built the house on Union Street in 1717 known now as the 1785 House. Many of his descendants bore the name Sarah and sur-names of Daggett, West, Allen, Manter, Dias and Merry.

Here in the cemetery we seniors eventually congregate about three graves arranged side by side, several rows from the road-way toward the left: On flaking dark gray slates - some split on their tops and gathering pebbles, acorns and old leaves - intri-cately carved angels float over the inscriptions for Isaac Chase - 1778, Mary Chase - 1746 and Elizabeth Chase, "about 16 years"

- 1719. The elder Chase opened the cemetery in the back of his property to receive the body of one of his children. It is hard to envision the lives that these folks lived in the 18th century on a remote island depending for the most part on their hands and wits to survive. I am reading in the journal of a physician, Leroy Yale, M.D., who practiced in Holmes Hole in the 1830's. His ability to alter the course of disease was almost nil, even though he lived a hundred years later than the first Chases. As Vineyard men and boys increasingly "went down to the sea in ships," they faced the hazards of the ocean far from their families, a lonely life, no more so than their wives' at home.

The first gravestone I see, even before I walk to the Chase's graves, is a tall granite monument topped by stone vase and flowers, below which a hand carved ship moves across the sea in full sail. The inscription reads, "There is sorrow on the sea," followed by the name Peter Cromwell - died at sea - Ship Gladiator -Born 1814 - 1853 and more verse, "But I said truly this is grief and I must bear it". Below are two more inscriptions: Peter T. Cromwell 1854 - 1939, Susan Cleveland 1832 - 1902. Peter's widow Susan had grief to spare. She not only was pregnant when she lost her ship captain husband but was left with three children to raise alone in the Greek revival house on the south side of State Road just below Delano. However, the census of 1870 reported her to be the fifth wealthiest woman in town, a testament to her survival skills developed during the lonely months when Peter was at sea according to Norton.

Before leaving this place I notice a solitary stone in the far north-west corner for Manuel Pedro - Died 1896 age 23 - Born in Flores Western Islands. I wonder if this last was a seaman far from home or one of the first Azorean immigrants who became such an important piece of the heritage of Martha's Vineyard.

This cemetery was not the only one for early colonists on the harbor. In 1770 Isaac Daggett opened a lot on his own holdings on the hill behind Main Street to bury his wife Abigail West Daggett. Although Isaac was a great grandson of Isaac Chase, his avoidance of the family cemetery gave rise to a tradition, according to Norton, that others in the village found their Chase neighbors "uppity." The single plot grew to be Proprietor's Cemetery, another private site on Centre Street, now maintained by The Town of Tisbury behind the town hall.

A relaxed walk for those not tired takes us back to Edgartown Road, through the woods to State Road and the Tisbury Senior Center where we started. The fascination of old cemeteries is now matched in my mind by the unfolding of island history as told by Jim Norton.

HOW TO GET THERE: Park in the vicinity of lower South Main Street. Walk up State Road, pass Causeway Road, turn left on Delano Road just before you reach Edgartown Road. At the end on the left is the Chase Cemetery. On leaving, retrace your steps on Delano Road to State Road, turn right downhill and return to Main Street.

I am indebted for much of the historical information here to "Walking in Vineyard Haven" by James H. K. Norton, Published by The Martha's Vineyard Historical Society, 2000.

Farm Pond

Ken Vincent

Farm Pond Preserve

Lilly, my springer and I ride to Trade Wind Fields Preserve in Oak Bluffs bound for Farm Pond Preserve, 27.5 acres acquired in 1989 and 1996 by the Town of Oak Bluffs and Martha's Vineyard Land Bank Commission. The pond adjoins Sea View Avenue and most of the preserve lies inland from the pond itself and connects by easements on Oak Bluffs Water Department property to the new Oak Bluffs School, and Trade Wind Fields where I've parked. A small section sits off Sea View Avenue with a view of Nantucket Sound just at the beginning of the bike path to Edgartown. Lilly's at home resting after a strenuous hike yesterday. I fear her age is catching up with her. My wife admonishes me to be careful not to take her too far afield.

First, I spray my shoes and pant legs with Permethrin to discourage ticks. They seem to be heavy this season and I've had Lyme Disease once which is enough. The trail map on the board directs me left on the blue trail at the large Trade Wind field and soon to another left on the yellow and I am on my way to Farm Pond taking another look at pitch pines this trip. Instead of disliking them as I did before because of their rough black bark, I've come to view them as hardy survivors in tough surroundings. They thrive in the wind and salt air on nothing much but sandy soil, preserve the water table in many places where rains might simply wash away and they provide cover for walkers like me who otherwise might burn from unblocked sun. I can see today another plant that thrives on sandy soil, poison ivy. Their small reddish green leaves, three together, are uncoiling from dormant winter vines. At this stage they are less recognizable than later when they unfurl completely.

The path is soft with its pine needle cover and signs announce the water company's boundaries. The spanking new Oak Bluffs School looms up at the edge of the woods. Its giant cupola must look out over the whole of the town. Kids are in the yard tossing balls, shooting baskets, running around full of joyful chatter. Soon I'm at the edge of an old grass plain, now threatened with "succession" by other grasses, weeds, brush and trees. The Norton family farmed this area from 1814 to 1888 followed by Manuel Bettencourt from 1889 to 1926. The land bank sign relates that in 1850 this land supported "60 sheep, 8 cattle, 2 cows and 4 oxen". Rye, corn, potatoes, and hay were harvested before farming was abandoned and land began to revert to the present growth of cedars, pitch pine and black cherry. The disappearance of many native grassland plants has resulted in a decline of natural habitat - moles, white footed mice, marsh hawks, brown owls and red tail hawks. Restorative management of this area is now underway. A cooperative venture between the land bank and the Oak Bluffs School has opened this whole area for children to experience their natural surroundings and to learn about their environment.

This is a place to wonder at. The quietness is surprising so close to the school and housing, none of which is in evidence. A wooden walkway leads out over the marsh to the edge of a tiny pond. The silence is broken by the burp of a Budweiser frog somewhere out there. I sit on the lower rail of the barrier and wait to see what happens by. I hear the familiar calls of one blackbird to another and see a tricolor on the tree nearest. Across the way, the other caller shoulders two bright red stripes. Tree swallows veer in and out searching for mosquitoes and other flying insects. Suddenly I hear the heavy patter of an animal's foot pads behind me on the walk and a huge tan mastiff pokes his head around the corner to nuzzle me. His owner, just behind, is interrupting her morning run along the trail. "Kaiser is only nine months old. I have to be careful not to run him too far because of his young hips," she says. The young woman and Kaiser resume their jog.

I've passed areas of tilled earth which I suspect represent a weeding out of unwanted species and the planting of others. Two nesting boxes for swallows or blue birds stand in the field to my left. Soon another walkway opens onto the inland shore of Farm Pond itself. The water is dark blue and mirror-like this morning. A sign forbidding shell fishing because of contamination is a surprise, perhaps not so surprising an indication of how close we are to spoiling the environment even when it is under conservation as this area is. Otherwise the pond appears pristine and peaceful. A swan sails by, a blue jay darts in and out of the bushes and a cardinal's red flash catches my eye as I rise from my relaxing break.

Continuing along the trail, I come too soon to the tarmac of South Circuit Avenue and debate with myself about hiking farther onto Sea View Avenue and around to the second short trail. It looks a good way over and, of course, I have to walk back. Something about the walk so far has relaxed me and I'm game for more. Joining Canonicus Avenue I enter onto Sea View Avenue. The bright blue of Nantucket Sound, all the way to Spain it seems, spreads out before me. If there is no other moment than this on the walk this morning, I am satisfied. There is something about the boundless sea that never loses its grandeur and surprise for me when I have been in the woods or a street in the town and suddenly encounter this endless blue all the way to the horizon.

Another quarter mile brings me beyond the beginning of the bike path to Edgartown. I pass the high sea wall on my left and over the little bridge where crabbing is a favorite sport in warm weather if the water is pure, to the land bank logo of part two of my walk. It is barely a hop and a skip into the woods at the side of the road to the edge of Farm Pond where a dozen Canada geese are nesting in the marshy grass. All heads are raised to quick attention with my intrusion. I watch for a while, glad that none flaps his wings and flies away. Heads are still attentive until I drift silently away and back to Sea View Avenue.

On my return to the preserve, my attention is caught again by the land bank sign, attesting to the presence of 180 different species of plant life on this small preserve. I have seen royal fern just uncoiling their fiddle backs. Sea lavender and butterfly weed will come later in the season. As the pond nears the edge of the dirt road I see cattails reaching up with their brown cylindrical heads. They made great torches soaked in kerosene when we found them as kids walking with my grandfather. Now, most of them have disappeared from the shores of Menemsha Pond in Chilmark because of the encroachment of phragmites grass. I see this foreigner is making inroads here also at the edge of the pond. Although it is tall and graceful, bearing a tasseled grassy head, it is notoriously invasive and eliminates many native species. A friend tells me there is some effort to eliminate this grass by the painstaking process of cutting it down and applying a retardant, stalk by stalk.

Some time back, I wondered if I would ever become jaded with my hiking these trails but for every walk I've been rewarded, never bored or disappointed. Today, everything I see, the birds, greening of plants, even poison ivy, but best of all, the boundless sea opening at the foot of Canonicus Avenue, keeps my spirit raised for more trailside adventures. As I walk back to my pick-up, I miss Lilly but, by compensation, will savor these two hours of enjoyment for the rest of the week.

HOW TO GET THERE: Park at the end of sea wall on Sea View Avenue in Oak Bluffs and walk toward Edgartown beyond the start of the bike path, enter the loop trail at the land bank logo on your right. Retrace your steps toward Oak Bluffs and turn left on Canonicus Avenue, walk about a quarter mile to enter trail at L.B. logo on your left. Or drive on County Road, Oak Bluffs, to the corner of Barnes Road at the fire house, turn east toward Oak Bluffs on Barnes Road, enter Pheasant Lane (2nd right), go to end, turn left, then right on Trade Winds Road by the wooden barrier and enter parking area for Trade Wind Fields on left at LB. logo. Follow blue trail to the left side of the large field, then left on yellow and follow signs. Be sure to keep the Oak Bluffs School on your left when you leave the woods. For each set of directions you retrace your steps to your car.

Ripley's Field

Ken Vincent

Ripley's Field and Wompesket

Two tries searching for Wompesket from Ripley Field and I am no nearer to this small gem of a Land Bank Preserve than George Mallory apparently was to the summit when he fell off a shelf on his hike to Mount Everest. At least my body is free to try again. One of the surprises about the increasing numbers of land set-asides on the Vineyard is how hidden from view and from consciousness they are for many Vineyarders. One of my friends built a home and lived actually within a quarter mile of Ripley's Field and has never been there.

Wompesket, Ripley's Field and Tisbury Meadow, three of the Land Bank's Preserves, in a way, are all of a piece. The bulletin board at the entrance to Ripley's Field tweaks my curiosity with the possibility of seeing a blue bird in the field - only a short walk in from the car - I seem to be the only grown person on Martha's Vineyard who's never seen a blue bird. My disappointment at finding the field bird-free is mitigated by the hope that the welcoming bird house on a pole will house a pair shortly. I vow to return. In early April I must be ahead of the season. Ripley's Field seems an anomaly - neatly cut and free of all but one or two trees. I catch my breath emerging from the cool woods into the bright sunshine. I didn't know this was here. My friend building a house didn't know either.

It is soon apparent that traffic over the years through the wooded surroundings has been frequent if not chaotic. A crisscrossing of ancient ways goes this way and that. Fortunately, the Land Bank has posted signs to identify Shubael Weeks Road, Road to Chappaquonsett, and Red Coat Hill Road. The last conjures up the story, perhaps apocryphal, of a handful of Revolutionary recruits marching round and round the top of a hill with wooden muskets atop shoulders, demonstrating to British war ships passing in nearby Vineyard Sound the presence of endless numbers of armed citizens waiting to repel the Red Coats should they dare land here.

The minimal guide map directs me to Red Coat Hill Road - beyond the preserve through private land - left to Tisbury Meadow, right to Wompesket. The trail markers end and I wend my way through pleasant woods and, as predicted, up a steep incline. Heavy tree growth to the north obstructs what I sense offered an eighteenth century view of the British ships passing in the Sound. Suddenly I am on a fine hard macadam road leading up hill past a house where deep throated dogs bark ominously. This must be the wrong way, my timid inner voice tells me and I retrace my steps.

At the bottom of the incline another unmarked way leads northwest. A small, very small, home-made wooden arrow with "W" beckons. Wompesket, of course, I say.

This also leads up hill and now, with thinner woods, the sun warms us. I've almost forgotten my springer, Lilly, trotting easily by my side. She's panting and looking up at me as if to say, give me a drink, boss. A still, opaque, mirror pond with occasional protruding dead tree trunks appears beyond a curve. Two black ducks float casually by. Lilly, now at the limit of her leash, splashes in and stands relaxing in the cool water. She laps some up in desultory manner - the cooling of her body now more urgent than her thirst. This road, too, leads among widely spaced private homes. Another sign at the foot of a drive gives away the previous anonymity of the sign marked "W". So much for Wompesket! With constant referring to my map and a one-hundred-eighty degree turn I take to go back, I am less sure of where I am. Did I pass that yard before with the truck and machinery or did I only see it as I turned from that path on my left? What a kick to be reported lost by supper time and humiliation at being rescued by the paramedics! The Road to Chappaquonsett sign erases doubts and Lilly and I return to the car. Next time we'll find that pesky Wompesket.

I return about the same time next year when there is no better time to take a quiet walk in the woods than on a this mild windless spring day unless it's a day or two after a good rainfall. The woods off Lambert's Cove Road in the Ripley's Field Preserve are absolutely quiet. Even my footfalls are silent on the moist velvet cushion of leaves on hard packed trail. The quick shudder of each footstep transmitted through bone to inner ear is the only locomotive indication to my senses that my body is actually moving along the path. The feeling is entirely within. Once in a while my springer, Lilly, kicks up a few loose leaves off the trail and generates a weak rendition of the usual leafy rustle of a walk in the woods. We are looking this morning for the lost Wompesket Preserve. My previous attempt resulted in a "pass" and I vowed, like MacArthur, to return. Ripley's Field has grown up a little since I last saw it. The steady intrusion of tiny pines on the perimeter is more evident this time. If blue birds were here last summer, they certainly are absent today. Three crows follow me as I re-enter the woods on the field's far side and follow me cawing one to the other until I am several hundred yards away from whatever they thought belonged to them. Once again the unmarked Road to Chappaquonsett takes me to the right and the intersection with Shubael Weeks Road. There, a sign placed by the Land Bank directs us through the intersection to Red Coat Hill Road, our main destination leading to Wompesket. The final approach to the top of Mott's Hill is a good climb and brings us to a bare skull cap of a summit spotted with several homes and barns. I look longingly toward Vineyard Sound, hoping to catch a glimpse of the sea where British frigates purportedly viewed the "massed" colonials marching round and round the top of the hill with wooden muskets. Even though the trees are mostly bare the Sound eludes me.

Taking our path over these ancient ways, found all over the woods of Lambert's Cove, reminds me of the past when travel was primitive and the early settlers drove their cattle and horses and walked themselves wherever they found the easiest access. Now these ways provide access to otherwise hidden and bounded areas off the beaten track. A connection from Ripley's Field and Wompesket exists because of the ancient ways here, a common inheritance from the past for these public trails and private homes alike. Except for the three dogs along the way who greet us with vociferous high-pitched barking, no one seems to mind our relative intrusion. Something I read a long time ago reassures me about barking dogs. When they bark in a high pitched howling, they are simply announcing and protecting their own territory. If I make no move to invade their sanctum, I'll pass unmolested. I say a little prayer as we pass with my hand in my pocket on a dog biscuit of which I have a store just for cases like this. The patch of hard tar road is only that and soon gives way to a sandy country road and, finally, a ground level Land Bank logo for Wompesket.

We walk up and down the peculiar eskers or small hills left by the glacier. Back in Ripley's Field Preserve differences of 70 feet are found between bottoms and peaks. At the bottoms the ground is a little marshy but passable. Here we enter some woods and lose sight of the several homes along the way but not before Lilly takes advantage of a small pond for a quick swim and drink to the accompaniment of several cackling fowl housed in a nearby barn. Here again, the silence and isolation from the rest of life on the Vineyard is startling. We have walked only a half mile from the border of Ripley's Field Preserve, yet we might as well be fifty miles away. No wonder that several hikers have admitted this is one of their favorite walks. The few cold nights of the past week seem to have dampened the appetites of deer ticks. We don't see a single one today and Wompesket is said to be notorious for them. The marshy borders of the path give way occasionally to a small rill spanned by thick planks or rudimentary bridges. A second loop of trail farther in takes us around an oval field of tall faded grasses. One lone wild cherry dares to take hold within the otherwise uniform grassy field. Soon my feet are wet in the spongy path. Recent rain has nowhere to run off. I can see gobs of clay along the path which will hold up the water from "percolating" down.

Our way back is marked only by the repeated howling of those dogs. If we continue past the junction of Red Coat Hill Road and Road to Chappaquonsett, we will emerge on State Road in Vineyard Haven just above Tisbury Meadow Preserve. I am tempted to turn onto Shubael Weeks Road to see where it comes out but we have had nearly an hour and a half of walking. I think we'd better return to the truck. During this entire period we meet only one other walker as we approach the end of the trail. Her springer with tight brown and white curls and an inquisitive nose for the biscuits in my pocket would love to play with Lilly if we remained longer.

HOW TO GET THERE: Wompesket has no available parking but can be reached either from Tisbury Meadow Preserve or Ripley's Field Preserve. Both require following Red Coat Hill Road. Directions are posted at the trail heads for each of the latter two preserves. All three are owned and maintained by Martha's Vineyard Land Bank. Ripley's Field: Drive 0.7 mi on lower Lambert's Cove Road. Turn left on John Hoft Road. Parking is a few hundred feet on the left. Tisbury Meadow: Drive up-Island on State Road 0.4 mi past Tashmoo Overlook. Turn into drive on left and park at the end to the left of the Mai Fain house.

Edgartown Light

Ralph Stewart

Edgartown Lighthouse Beach

The season is advancing and the grandkids will soon be here looking to explore a place they've never seen before. Even though a northeast wind blows at 15 to 20 knots and the temperature is more like roaring March than late April, I call a friend and propose a walk. Gloria says she rises early so I phone her a couple of minutes after seven. She's raring to go. At the end of Fuller Street in Edgartown we park, the only car on the street. Carpenters banging nails can be heard down the beach a-ways where new wheat-colored shingles adorn a huge beach side home gleaming in its new coat of cedar.

The original Edgartown Lighthouse was built in 1828 and stood on a small sand island, accessible only by boat at the entrance to the harbor. The present one which we approach along the beach with the wind at our backs was barged over from Cape Cod and erected on the same site in 1938. By this time sand had filled in the gap between shore and island and the new light stood on shore. In days past it provided safe warning of rocks and shoals to seamen sailing along the eastern shore of the island.[1] The beach at low tide, like it is today, is broad and sandy, much of it littered with thousands of shells. The descent into water appears gradual and smooth, too chilly today but a welcome romp I suspect in summer. Beyond to our right lie the

1 Now a relic of a bygone era, a more recent development has rescued this particular light from obscurity. The renovated base will be paved with over a hundred granite cobblestones, each bearing the name of a child, "taken from us too young, too early," says John Budris, author of the program note for the "Children's Memorial Lighthouse Dedication," July 14, 2001. The subscription for these memorial stones has been high according to the Martha's Vineyard Historical Society, present steward of Edgartown Light.

town and the harbor curving south out of view to Katama. In summer, boats of all description will sail in and out just in front of where we stand in front of the light. We catch a good sideways look at the Harborview Hotel in all its Victorian glory. I count eight conical spires at roof line and suspect I may be missing some on the back side.

Ahead we see the Chappaquiddick Beach Club and the multi-colored bath houses. One of my first visits to Chappy was on a day when President Kennedy and Jackie were anchored off the beach and swam with their guests in the calm protected water. Far out to the left juts Cape Pogue's elbow into Nantucket Sound. I make out the faint outline of a tall thin windmill, even the delicate blades rotating on top. Gloria spies the dwarfed Cape Pogue Light with its triangular black cap. We turn into the wind to head back toward the north where Cape Cod lies in a bit of haze. Now our trudging is heavier but Gloria, head down, is preoccupied with what she finds on the shore. She produces from her pocket a plastic bag and into it she collects all manner of shells and stones. "I love to collect these things," she says. "When I get home I examine each one, feel its surface and enjoy its unique shape and texture."

Suddenly I'm seeing something interesting and bend over to pick up a perfect moon shell and a broken bit of gray stone resembling an Indian bird point. The stones on the beach, almost all small and smooth, have a remarkable quality, some the weight of paper and almost as thin. The sea must have taken years to achieve this degree of abrading and polishing.

The wind makes my ears ache. I'm glad I thought to bring gloves but a summer Red Sox cap barely covers my head, nothing to pull down to my neck. Clouds in the distance are thick and gray but rain is not in the air. We're intrigued by the heavy cement work along some of the shore beyond a small narrow strip of water trapped by the sandy beach. It would appear that docking facilities once stood almost under the front porches of some of the large cottages. The shore has built up and made the facilities obsolete, a reminder of older days of private docks and large yachts directly at the foot of green lawns.

Much of the beach to the north is roped off to protect the nesting piping plovers and sand dune restoration. By this time we've accumulated an assortment that will drive me to my Zim and Ingle's "Seashores" to identify whelks, sea slippers, moon shells, false angels, along with the familiar soft shell clams, quahogs, razor clams and scallops. There is not a place I go it seems I don't find something new, here today shells and odd rocks, other times birds or trees or glacial debris. Gloria fishes another plastic bag from a pocket and hands me her full one to carry. "I come prepared," she says. Not content, I continue to add to her full bag while she keeps picking. We come to the narrow spit of sand which extends out toward the sea pointing more east than north and ends with waves lapping its tip, the end of our beach reaching out to protect Eel Pond. To our left, the northwest, lies the pond, actually a sheltered cove of the ocean. The bushes and trees on the far shore of Edgartown mark out Sheriff's Meadow Sanctuary, the first of its kind established by Henry Hough, past owner and editor of the Vineyard Gazette for over sixty years.

Sudden screeching directs us to two birds hurtling by, their sharply marked wings in white and their plump bodies seeming to skim through the air as easily as their more svelte cousins, the terns and gulls, we see more commonly. In addition to these, we count another pair of American oyster catchers this morning, confirmed by a knowledgeable looking woman who pauses to say hello on our way back. Her binoculars and ready answer to my inquiry establishes her expertise without doubt.

We enjoy the relief of walking with the wind at our backs as we return to the car. I have found a new exploration for the grandkids and Gloria has introduced me to another source of collectibles, a proper close to a bracing spring walk at Edgartown Lighthouse Beach.

HOW TO GET THERE: In-season parking is very difficult in Edgartown. Most certain is to drive to the Triangle and take public transportation to Kelly Lane in the center of town, walk out North Water Street to the Harborview Hotel, admiring the old whaling homes in the historic district along the way. Across from the hotel a path leads you to the lighthouse and beach. Off-season, two public lots near the Yacht Club and the Kelly House and some time-restricted on-street parking are available. Be sure to observe the restrictions on the beach for the protection of nesting birds and dune restoration.

Felix Neck   Ralph Stewart

Felix Neck Wild Life Sanctuary

Springtime has gained momentum over the past three weeks. Pinkletinks fill the evening air with their rasping high pitched vibrations. The number of different plant species blooming increases with each week: crocuses, snow drops, grape hyacinths and daffodils. A crowd of blue star flowers covers the front lawn of a house on the Edgartown Road in West Tisbury. On a cool blustery morning during the last week of Standard Time I am heading toward Felix Neck Wild Life Sanctuary where Gus Ben David has agreed to meet me for a walk.

Felix Neck, named for a Native-American named Felix Kuttashamaquat living here in the mid 1660's, is a 350 acre wild life sanctuary on the shore of Sengekontacket Pond behind State Beach in Edgartown. The Smith family farmed this land since the early 1800's and George Moffet, Jr. bought the land in 1963, intending it to become a nature preserve. The first summer nature camp began in 1964 as Fern and Feather under auspices of Martha's Vineyard Natural History Society. In 1969 Gus Ben David hired on as sanctuary director and Mr. Moffet began his generous donation of the whole area to the Massachusetts Audubon Society. The sanctuary's programs and development have grown hand in hand over the years under Gus's guidance. The Martha's Vineyard Commission describes the area as the Vineyard's premier environmental education center.

Gus's enthusiasm for Felix Neck knows no bounds. He punctuates our walk with a steady flow of information and observations. "These trails are laid out with precision," he says. "Each one's color coded and we ask visitors to study the sign board at the visitor's center to be sure they know where to go." This morning we begin on the Jessica Hancock Memorial Trail to the southeast and stop by a tiny pond partly hidden by dense brush. "We have a healthy population of spotted turtles in here. They're on an endangered list by the state."

"How do you know they're healthy?" I ask.

"We trap the fledglings and observe their numbers and activity."

"Look at that black bird. What a beautiful site. See the red wing bars," says Gus. Obvious, I think, when you know about these things. The trails are neat as a pin and recent cutting into the encroaching brush on either side ensures continued easy walking on a wide expanse of grass. "We had a wonderful donation some time ago," Gus says. "I'll show you the new golf cart we have back at the center. Now, if a grandmother comes to Felix Neck with her grandchildren for a morning program, she may say her arthritis is too bad to do the trails. I bring out the cart and take her around anywhere she wants while the kids are busy. I park it right up here to the side. She looks out over that marsh and sees everything. Even young mothers can wheel their babies around these smooth paths."

We approach the very edge of the marsh looking out over to Sarson's Island and the State Beach. "Wait a minute," exclaims Gus. "What's that swan doing walking around over there?" He brings the field glasses to his face. "No, not a swan; it's an egret, a common. See the yellow bill. In Florida there's another bird looks just like this, the white form of the blue heron. Not a separate species, just a morph." The word metamorphosis runs through my mind.

"You mean," I ask, "the Florida bird you mentioned is like an albino great blue heron, the morph?" Gus nods his head. I think he agrees but probably is leaving room for further interpretation of the exact nature of a morph. I'm satisfied I know enough. I've already seen a blackbird and some goldfinches, crows and grackles. A coughing noise, somewhat muffled, comes up from the edge of the marsh and a large bird takes flight. "Great blue heron," Gus says, swinging his glasses around to follow her. "She gave you her typical call."

In a few moments another sound, more like a squeak, comes from the trees. "What's that, another heron?" I ask.

"No, Gus replies, "only a couple of branches rubbing on each other."

We join the Orange Trail and come to the observation blind, a place I remember from years gone by when I came with my children to watch ducks. It looks just the same although the water's higher than I remember. What I haven't remembered is that this is a tidal pond connected by a thin channel to the salt marsh beyond. The water level rises and falls. Three Canada geese, several mallards float by. "The yellow-eyes and buffle heads have all gone," Gus observes. "They've headed up north already." Even on this early spring day the sun striking the little deck of the observation blind is warm enough to encourage a long period of sitting outside and watching the activity in the pond. "This is a place to sit and just wait for nature to come to you," Gus says, almost reading my mind about what I'd like to do. We move on and join the Old Road which in times past led to the point of Felix Neck jutting out into Sengenkontacket. Clarence Smith lived in a cabin near the end of the road and fished the ponds, leading a reclusive life for many years according to reports. He died one day in the pond dragging for scallops, Gus tells me. His old shell heaps are still discernible under the leaves and rotting forest floor nearby.

"Look at that muskrat," says Gus as he stops and wheels back a step. There's nothing I can see at first. Looking closely at the edge of the path I see a flat carapace of matted fur covered with miniature bleached bones of various shapes. I recognize vertebra the size of small signet rings and a haphazard arrangement of the rest. "Probably killed by a hawk," Gus says.

"Head's gone. We leave things like this just the way we find them for the youngsters to see and study. That way they learn about the life of the sanctuary." My temptation to brush the mess aside evaporates and, for the first time ever, I look at the lifeless remains of a creature as a thing of hidden beauty.

Around a sharp turn in the path we arrive at Elizabeth's Pond, sheltered from the wind, clear and dark. Like Water Fowl Pond we've just visited and one to come, it is a man-dug pond in an area once occupied by low swampy ground. A side trail takes us to the edge of Major's Cove on the northeast side of Felix Neck. Almost directly opposite is Pecoy Point where I watched a fisherman harvest oysters last summer. Here on this side is one of the favorite spots for youngsters and their teachers during the summer season of Fern and Feather. They can snorkel, swim and collect specimens for their study of aquatic life. The water is deep blue today. We think the residents across the way to the west must view this quiet shore with the pleasure of knowing it will be wild forever.

We come to Turtle Pond. "Once these swampy areas were dug out," Gus tells me, "the ponds filled up and native animals and water life just moved in. Look, over by that rock, see the muskrat swimming along." The trees overhead are just beginning to bud out. Even the beetlebungs, appearing almost certainly dead all winter, have tiny buds. We leave the muskrat trying to climb up on a large rock in the middle of the pond. "That long board out there is for the turtles to sun themselves and let the tourists, especially the kids, have a good look." Gus smiles. I sense he feels this pond and the rest of Felix Neck are his babies. The years haven't dimmed his enthusiasm.

"I've grown up here on the Vineyard," Gus reminisces. As a kid I used to drive by State Beach and look over Sengenkontacket and wonder what this place was like. Now, after all these years, I've had the pleasure of working the land

and helping to preserve it for Island kids and visitors to enjoy - enjoy the unspoiled land and learn about nature."

We're back at the Visitors Center. "Thanks for the walk and the talk, Gus," I say. We shake and I head for my pick-up. Instead of driving off, I sit on the tail gate in the sun looking out toward the tall pole where an osprey seems to be rearranging last year's nest. Seventy or eighty smaller poles holding tree swallow houses dot the landscape. They should be occupied in the next week or two. The field in front of me is much larger than on my last visit. Gus has been working a long time on these fields. Finally, I drive off wishing I could stay longer. I pause at the main gate to look at the boulder which Ann Hale describes in "Marsh to Moraine" as a ventifact, a boulder shaped and burnished by severe winds at the time of the last glacier. One sharply slanted surface is almost as smooth as paper. Another surface, the "heel", is rough and irregular. I head home on the Vineyard Haven Road, hoping I can return for the Osprey Festival on Saturday, April 8.

HOW TO GET THERE: Drive 2 miles from the intersection of Barnes Road (airport road) and Vineyard Haven-Edgartown Road. Turn left onto the sandy road at the Audubon logo for Felix Neck Sanctuary.

SUMMER

After the slow emergence of spring, cold easterly rains and a canopy explosion over oak woods, town streets take on the leafy green of new maples. Lilacs bloom in yards and along the roads. Dogwoods spread their branches over upper Main Street in Vineyard Haven, at the bottom of North Road in West Tisbury and within fenced in greenswards along the neat grid of streets in downtown Edgartown. At long last, although only a minute it seems since last Labor Day, summertime has come to the Vineyard. Ferries shuttle back and forth without cease bearing the human increase native islanders know as summer folks, friends and neighbors missed over the long winter but who return as predictably as the fourth of July just around the corner. Neighborhoods fill up and lights glow late in evenings, well past the time when off-season streets are dark by nine. Cars fill every space and the old question of traffic at five corners in Vineyard Haven and parking in all towns return as topics of the day. A writer to the Times demands a traffic light at Airport Road which in turn provokes a spate of outrage at the mere mention of such a "mainland" perversion of island life – unthinkable. And so the cars pile up and tempers shorten as summer progresses.

I was seduced in mid-June years ago by the blue sky and water, the white wake of the Islander and the sails breezing along into Vineyard Sound. I was among the horde who spread out from the dock at the foot of Union Street into Vineyard Haven and eventually during two or three weekends explored the perimeter and the midlands of the island. The crowds were exciting and the exodus on a Sunday evening became a ritual;

the clank of the car over the transfer bridge into the dank ferry hold became the pattern of the landlubber's sea journey if only seven miles, never far from landfall, to Woods Hole. And then I became a full-time resident and never looked back in regret.

The excitement of summer has never ended. I welcome the noisy clamor of chattering seniors leaving their busses. My increasing age is modified in spirit by the arrival of younger and younger visitors. The average age of the Vineyard decreases in my eyes at least by a decade and a half after July 4th until it reverts toward its more senior-oriented mean by October. True, the traffic is beyond belief, mopeds are only slightly worse than bicycles on our narrow roads and the emergency room at Martha's Vineyard Hospital does a busy trade in accidents of all kinds. I wish at times that visitors would enjoy relaxing and doing nothing more than they do but they project a kindness (with a few exceptions), a curiosity about our life here and, to be frank, tolerate the increased price of gasoline and school taxes with exceeding grace.

However, summer brings unusual stress to Vineyarders who make a living on a short summer season. When I practiced medicine, I could anticipate a flurry of local patients in mid August who wondered why they felt under par, tired, yet sleepless, and afraid they were developing serious ailments. Most were simply over worked and stressed. Labor Day guaranteed them relief.

Visitors and native Vineyarders now are discovering trails they never imagined to exist - out of sight, hidden along country roads, along meadows and streams, up hills and down dales, reaching vistas of the south shore or Vineyard Sound, all providing relief from noise and traffic and worries of home and job. Walking and exploring begin whenever a Vineyarder develops the yen and they can continue through the year for anyone lucky enough to visit or live here year-round. I pass easily from the hubbub of downtown Edgartown or Oak Bluffs to the woods which lead to an overlook of a great marsh and salt pond. I shake off the doldrums of a rainy day visit with grandchildren to the relaxing walk next day in the sun with the same kids freed up to explore a trail and discover at its end a refreshing swim on the north shore. I muse by myself about the wonders of nature along a sandy strip of beach while watching sanderlings skitter up and down the waves feeding on crustaceans and mollusks. Summer climaxes the Vineyard year and I'm glad I'm here.

View from Peaked Hill   Tyson Trish

Peaked Hill Reservation

Fluffy mashed potato clouds scud up from the northwest on a hazy Saturday morning as faithful springer, Lilly, and I set out for Peaked Hill in Chilmark. It's pre-season June and traffic on the roads and at the Chilmark Store near Beetlebung Corner is already mounting. Peaked implies rising to a peak. In fact, Little Peaked Hill, site of the old Army Signal Corps radar station is 308 feet, while its close northern neighbor Peaked Hill itself is 311 feet, neither a strain on oxygen supply or pressure on the middle ear. I suppose the highest hills on the Vineyard deserve the term peaked although that's a little stretch. The American Heritage Dictionary pronounces "peaked" as pea-kid, a surprise to me. I thought that referred only to the condition of feeling or looking pea-kid, also spelled p-e-a-k-e-d. I would never dare call a tall thin house pea-kid, rather the unisyllabic peaked as in peeked for looking around corners surreptitiously. Lilly isn't interested in discussions of words or their pronunciation so we move on to the actual walk this morning. I enter Tabor House Road, the "dump road", on the left off Middle Road from Chilmark Center. Another half mile brings me to a dirt road on the left with the discrete white sign of Martha's Vineyard Land Bank. Radar Hill itself was purchased in 1975 by the Vineyard Open Land Foundation, and the rest, the bulk of the preserve today comprising seventy acres in hilly upland, by the Martha's Vineyard Land Bank Commission in 1992. Bearing always right I find the small car park and trail head at the 0.7 mile mark.

Already the day is becoming brighter. The land bank bulletins seem always to throw down the challenge to bird watchers (50 species already identified here) and to botanists (170 plant species known and catalogued) for the unwary walker. A distinct ringing of a phone startles me into realizing we must not be so far from civilization as I would have guessed by the distance we've traveled in from the tar road. In fact, the sound is so close I look over at my red truck to see if Ford has installed a signal somewhere I have not heard before. Obviously the ringing comes from just beyond the drop from the parking lot and the tree line. We enter tall oak woods and start along the blue trail. Light slants in from the left above. Shadows play on the trail ahead. The phone has stopped and we are once more alone along the central ridge passing east to west on the Vineyard. We are actually walking on old car tracks in a grassy road but soon veer off to the left on a single-file path marked blue. A state of relaxation and dreaminess actually begins to take over. Lilly sniffs aggressively at the growth along the side. A little rise passes almost unnoticed until the trees suddenly thin out and we are on the crest of a steep declivity where the tall tree tops have sunk below eye level ahead of us. Beyond that lush green expanse is a view that awakens all my senses at once. We look over the mist-shrouded view to Menemsha, Lobsterville, Cutty Hunk, Nashawena and Woods Hole away to the east. We've seen this view before at Cedar Tree Neck but here at Peaked Hill the out-look is unique in itself, all the more arresting because of its sudden appearance brinked at the steep decline in front of us. We walk to the natural rock platform and drink in the distance. The mist doesn't hide the view as much as it augments a surreal sense of looking into an exotic and mysterious sea just discovered. A steep path down takes us around and back to the east with the look-out now above us and out of sight. The drought this year has not affected the greenery but keeps the flying insects to a minimum. What goes down must come up, to reverse the old saying, and we clamber up a steep incline and turn left on the orange trail through more high oaks to the Stonecutters Rock. Enormous slabs of granite lie on their sides against a free-standing boulder of immense size. One of the supine slabs clearly has been worked by human guided chisels. What could the purpose have been? How long ago? Had the slabs been brought here from a distance and who might have performed such a Herculean task? I could make no sense of it. The name is good enough. I can accept the mystery.

A little further we come to Wee Devil's Bed. Bette Carroll later tells me there is a "real" devil's bed around here. (I presume she means a grown-up adult devil. I would like to see his bed but not today.) The flat top of this erratic glacial boulder is scooped out as if to record the impress of some small giant's posterior on the oblong rock-hard mattress. It holds the remainder of the light rain we had two days ago. This was to become an important part of Lilly's walk later today.

Turning right from orange to yellow trail we ascend again to the edge of the woods and emerge from under the oak canopy. Thirty-five years ago I came to this spot up the macadam road off Middle Road before there were any houses along the way. The old radar station still stood but barely. Long deserted and weather-invaded, a couple of ramshackle buildings survived the elements. The intriguing feature was the embankment of old sandbags, burlap long gone in the winds but the sand still, incredibly, holding the original form previously contained within the burlap sacks. The memory of WWII was a little fresher then and I could imagine the look-outs standing guard, feeling wind-blown and their desolation in this place. [A return visit a few months later would find these buildings and sand embankments had been removed as a beautification effort for the reservation, leaving only remnants of some old uneven macadam and a few cement retaining walls with iron protruding. The hill top was reverting to nature.] Once I had taken in my footing and the surrounding growth I saw belatedly the panorama of one-hundred-eighty degrees - from the long expanse of the south shore toward Edgartown to Noman's Land, and Gay Head. I remember the talk of building houses up here. I'm glad the Open Land Foundation started its preservation effort when it did.

Crossing the old macadam we follow a sandy path down a steep decline through low bush and emerge at the edge of a man-made meadow now overgrown with grass and weeds. A fire pond evidently has gone dry leaving a shallow depression in the far corner of the field. This area was left by the real estate developers who had hoped to make the meadow one of the "amenities" for the residents. Reading between the lines of the bulletin board at trail head, I think the land bank would agree with me that this ill- conceived idea should give way to a more appropriate use of the land.

Lilly suddenly stops and sets her legs against me as I lead with the leash. She seems to be avoiding taking the next few steps out of the shade into the now bright and warming sun light. Her tongue lolls from the side of her mouth and her breathing is rapid and shallow. You're too hot I think and we without any water. Best we rest in the shade a bit. And we do. I search over a slight rise for the fire pond but see no water. Soon enough, Lilly recovers and we take a short cut over the red trail back to the blue toward the car. She pulls a mule again on me just past Wee Devil's Bed. Obviously she remembers the shallow puddle and dampness under the oak shade. We clamber up again on the devil's bed and she laps a few mouthfuls before lying down full stretch in the cooling water. What a good master I have, her eyes tell me she is thinking. A whole bowl-full of water awaits her at the car.

HOW TO GET THERE: Take the State Road (South Road) up-Island to Beetlebung Corner in Chilmark Center. Bear right and immediately take the sharp right onto Middle Road which starts you back down-island for about a mile to Tabor House Road on the left. The entrance to the Peaked Hill Trail is on the left of Tabor House Road as you go toward the North Road, 0.5 miles from Middle Road. Follow the dirt road 0.7 miles, bearing right at each intersection. Turn right at the Open Land Foundation sign and park in the small area reserved at the trail head. A map of the trails is posted on the bulletin board and hand-held maps under plastic are available to borrow while you walk.

Middle Road Sanctuary

photos by Ralph Stewart

Middle Road Sanctuary

Driving down-Island on Middle Road in Chilmark two miles from Beetlebung Corner, I see for the first time ever the green sign of Sheriff's Meadow for Middle Road Sanctuary. How many times have I traveled Middle Road and not seen this place before? Learning from the past couple of walks, I now carry a small backpack loaded with two water bottles, one large for Lilly and one smaller for myself. Also rattling around with the bottles is a metal bowl for Lilly and mosquito repellent for me. She drinks from the bottle if I pour but most of it goes onto the ground. She takes a good drink from the bowl before we leave the side of the truck and start out on the red trail. A few steps farther, at a fork, we take the right hand loop of what turns out to be a full circle joining at the top to the yellow trail which should take us the rest of the way through to the end. I hesitate as we meet an old cart track not listed on the map which seems to head off to the right away from the loop. I choose to stick to the left on the loop.

Another choice soon faces me, a well worn path to the right seeming to go down in the direction of the path on the map, but there's no marker. I choose the right hand trail, and after a very pleasant walk down a long decline, end up at the foot of a drive-way to a private home. Beyond this leads to an intersection of dirt roads obviously going into several private areas. I think back to my Army experience, the marches and map reading exercises. I also think with some chagrin of the time, with my wife in the passenger seat, I puzzled over a road map trying to find my way through the streets of Springfield to Uncle Lloyd's nursing home. "Just stop and ask someone," Mary Ann had said. It's no problem to reclimb the hill, I say to myself, and continue on to find the end of the loop with the yellow marker for the correct trail just a few steps beyond the wrong turn.

The term "Sanctuary" chosen by Sheriff's Meadow for all its areas is especially apt for this one on Middle Road. It is one of the most serene preserves we've walked. These are the tallest trees I've seen on the Vineyard, giant black oaks and white oaks providing a high canopy little mixed with other tree species. The day is quiet, with clear air. I feel enclosed, yet free to wool-gather, with little intrusion from the outside except for the occasional chickadee's low and slow "chick-a-dee-dee-dee" and a distant crow's "caw-caw" while Lilly noses about in the blueberry foliage along the trail. I'm back in my mind's eye to the woods off Anthony's Beach Road in Padanaram when I was 11. I'm walking in similar woods on a cool early spring afternoon with Pete, my friend whom I follow everywhere like a small puppy. He has a BB gun from Christmas and we take turns shooting at crows. Never hit one, just hear their raucous cries and see their floppy flight as the small noise of the gun startles them into the air.

Another time later my son, Rusty, and another young friend and I are silently ensconced against a large oak somewhere just north of the Chilmark town dump. It is 4 am of a chill December morning and we wait for a deer to wander through our stand. The stars show through occasional gaps in the bare branches above. The sun waits a long, long time to silver the eastern sky. Since I am designated dresser-of-the-kill this morning, I am half-hearted in hopes of success. Our feet grow cold as we listen to scattered footfall of mice in the leaves at the base of trees. Distant muffled voices come over the hill, then veer off. My regret now is not so much that we didn't even see a deer that morning but that I didn't spend more such mornings with Rusty.

Lilly and I head downhill again, this time on the correct path, following a stone wall to our left. We are once more traveling across the irregular ridge or spine which passes east and west along the central Vineyard. Trees thin out a bit and we are aware of private homes coming up on the left. Finally a huge, erratic boulder, 8 to 10 feet high, left by the last glacial tumbling, comes into view. Beyond this "Overlook Rock" a vista unfolds of the Vineyard's south side and Tisbury Great Pond separated from the sea by its slender barrier dunes. The picture is tightly framed by rock and tree branches at the edge of the woody, sloping trail where we stand. I reluctantly heed the warning at trail-head not to trespass off the Sanctuary. The temptation to pass through the gate is almost too much, seeing that the small path through the gate is worn bare by frequent foot falls. The closed gate, official boundary marker, and "No Trespassing" sign all together are clear warnings.

Just beyond, we find another clearing in the trees and sit for a while on a sturdy bench to look out over Chilmark Pond and the vast south side. Sheriff's Meadow acquired the Sanctuary in 1968. I dare say the view from this trail in the earlier days was more spectacular than it is now. I've noticed how much Vineyard open land has become covered with dense growth in the 40 years I've lived here. Down we go again after sampling the drinks in my pack and giving Lilly a chance to lie down. She's so faithful. I think she'd follow me anywhere; I must be careful with her. At the bottom of this path we come to an ancient dirt road called King's Highway. It looks almost as well traveled as Flander's Lane in Chilmark, where I pass daily, but we meet no one. Instead of retracing our route back, we turn left on the ancient way and in about 15 minutes find ourselves on Meetinghouse Road. Another left heads us back to Middle Road. We rest, sitting at the edge of the road with our water as a sweaty jogger rolls by. The sun has heated up even the shade.

The hot trudge along the dusty road seems a great distance and, once turning left on Middle Road, the 0.4 mile back to our parking spot finds us both flagging. This alternate return route is 1.5 miles, barely more than retracing the way in to King's Highway. The weather forecast prompted my choice of today for this walk. Warm but clear with return to excessive temperatures and high humidity tomorrow. I'm glad I chose today. It's hot enough. I'm drenched through my hat band and T-shirt. Lilly's tongue lolls despite two other sit-down stops while she exhausts her large bottle of water and I my smaller one. Tomorrow will be worse. Good planning, Russ.

HOW TO GET THERE: From Chilmark Center at
Beetlebung Corner, start down-Island on Middle Road. At 1.2
miles, turn right at the green Sheriff's Meadow sign (Hough
Lane) into the parking lot for Middle Road Sanctuary. From
down-Island, go to West Tisbury Center on State Road, turn
right past Alley's Store onto Music Street. Take the first paved
road on your left, Middle Road, and proceed 2.4 miles until
you see the green Sheriff's Meadow sign on your left and turn
in to park.

Fulling Mill Brook   Tim Johnson

Fulling Mill Brook Preserve

Lilly's muzzle is warm against my thigh on the front seat and I suspect she's dreaming of rabbits and wild turkeys. The day is warm and clear as we turn right on easy-to-miss Henry Hough Lane and immediately turn aside on the left to the trail-head parking for Fulling Mill Brook Preserve, owned and managed by the Land Bank and Town of Chilmark. The little brook springs from somewhere north of the Middle Road but gathers small tributaries along the way from the marshy areas all along the trail here. I've always stumbled over the name Fulling Mill Brook. Somehow it seems more likely to be Fulling Brook Mill or there has been a mistake and it should be rendered Fulling Hill Mill, a little more euphonious to the ear.

I've discovered in the Britannia (an ancient form of encyclopedia for those who know only the Internet and such things as Netscape and Infopedia) what fulling really means. Here on the Vineyard it was a process in the manufacture of wool cloth, especially felt, a century ago but can refer to the processing of any type of cloth which may or may not include wool; it usually does. Fulling involves layering fibers together, one layer at a time, carding at least one layer at right angles to the others to produce "cross" in the batt and dimensional stability to the finished material. Subjecting the resulting batt to more water or acid, steam and pressure further melds the fibers in a tough adhesive bond. Once this felt is formed, it is then subjected to further washing and pounding in a mechanical chamber, steamed and shrunk. The shrinking, up to fifty per cent in the size of the batt, is probably the exact definition of fulling as that part of the total process of felt making. Charlie Parton, my old medical college classmate, tells me that woven woolen cloth is subjected to water and mild turbulence, as in a washing machine, for just a few minutes to effect shrinkage (or to be fulled) to a more uniform and dense weave, warmer for the wearer or sleeper.

And so Lilly and I begin our exploration of the Fulling Mill Brook, now deeply etched in my consciousness for what that little stream did in ancient days past. Of course, dammed up down-stream, it provided the power for the mill to do its work. Beyond these salient features I remain a little bit in the dark as to other details. As in so many processes involving the manufacture of textiles and the processing of wool, complicated is the operative adjective.

After initial realization of the old utilitarian existence of the brook, my mind is occupied with the close association of so much of the technological advance in the early days of the 18th and 19th centuries with rude natural resources we have come to see in quite a different light at the close of the twentieth century. I don't think of a small country brook as a source of energy. Those sources are far away, in Canada, producing our electricity which snakes across the country-side over tall steel high-tension towers, or else from tightly guarded nuclear energy sites often picketed by the Green people and pointed at for children to note the dangers of our atomic age. Ordinarily this small brook would be viewed in its purely esthetic sense: its cool calm on a hot day, the tinkle of its soft music when it ventures near the trail or flows under one of the man-made granite bridges over which we walk, or the relief it provides Lilly to her hot paws and underbelly. She actually balks at being led out of her bath half-way along the trail. I think of the pleasure I feel watching Charlie Parton as he spins the first strands of wool yarn on his peddle-operated wheel. He is capturing some of the old ways at Farmer's Market on Saturdays just as I do today envisioning the use of Fulling Mill Brook a century ago.

The man-made wooden bridges and causeways over difficult terrain are unobtrusive and give the sense of a well-tended treasure. Three granite bridges over the meandering stream survive from the days of the old mill. A momentary glimpse of the south side surf jumps out through a break in the tall trees and shrubs during the traverse over the green trail, a quick teaser and reminder of the southerly direction we're walking.

The end of the trail, now close to South Road by the sounds of the summer traffic, is as much a treat as the more secluded peaceful areas we've already passed through.. Facing the end at the side of South Road, is a stout gateway of Vineyard stone, the entrance to the old fulling mill itself. The bulletin board beyond the gate reminds us of some history of this preserve. Richard Pough, lifelong orthnithologist, who lives just east of the preserve, first encouraged the preservation of this area in the 1980's. He is one of the founders of the Nature Conservancy and wrote Audubon's Guide to Eastern Land Birds. He also helped found the Vineyard Conservation Society. The late Ed Chalif of Chilmark, a dedicated amateur scientist, conducted bird walks for years here and taught many of the local bird experts, Gus Daniels, Allan Keith, Susan Whiting, and Vern Laux. With Roger Tory Peterson, he wrote, "Birds of Mexico."

As we retrace our steps, we recross the third and largest rock bridge. I am amazed it sits 12 to 15 feet up from the slough which it spans for about twenty feet.. It is hard for me to see through the dense brush below whether the stream in fact passes under. I assume it does although the current drought may have reduced its volume of flow. A little to the west, the left on our return near this bridge, is a short path directly to the stream. There, a conglomeration of huge boulders and a broad earthen berm on each side of the stream apparently mark the site of an old dam, which, as my Flender's guide describes, at one time held back the water from which the power to run the mill was drawn. The glacier left these boulders at its most southern excursion, here, not so far from the sandy outwash we can walk along on the southern beaches.

Re-walking the trail I pay more attention to the trees and purity of the brook., "Successional" shrubs and trees begin to overtake the fields. Photographs from the thirties show much of this area to have been bare of trees. However, back at more northerly reaches of the preserve, sixty-foot high oaks and maples, some of which are said to be a hundred years old, shade the paths and brook.

I meet two women getting out of a car with Pennsylvania plates back at the parking area. How are the ticks, one asks after agreeing with me about the beautiful day. None today or the other day as far as I can see, I reply. Lilly didn't pick up any either, I add, as I inspect her black and white form on the front seat. She has collapsed already, waiting for another drink from her bottle of water. Where have they all gone, the lady asks. I think she doesn't quite believe me although my bare legs are obviously free of little black things as far as she must be able to see. They often leave this time mid-summer, I reply, but they'll be back in September. Keep up your guard but have a nice walk. This is a lovely place.

HOW TO GET THERE: Drive to Chilmark Center on State Road and turn right just past the Community Center and Library which are on the left. Then turn almost immediately right at the beetle bung grove onto Middle Road. Travel 1.2 miles and turn right on Hough Lane and follow Land Bank logo to parking on left.

Great Rock Bight   Susan Safford

Great Rock Bight Preserve

I have new companions for a walk: two grandsons, Corey, 9, Conor, 11, and a neighbor, Lee, 9, visiting from Madison, Wisconsin. We are bound for Great Rock Bight Preserve, 28 acres in Chilmark acquired in 1997 by Martha's Vineyard Land Bank. The dirt road in from North Road passes about a half mile through well kept woodlands. Here and there we pass a pasture walled in with stone, an occasional house or barn. I have the impression that the owners have tended this land with loving care over a long time. Preston Harris and his family have been synonymous with this section of upper North Road for several generations. I've seen Preston walking one of the pastures on previous visits.

The boys have about run out of patience during the fifteen minutes since we left home. They are action-oriented. I attempt to tease them into having an educational morning. It is, of course, a risky business. "I'll pay you fifty cents for each tree or bush you can identify and any animal or bird that you see and can name. Of course, I have to confirm what you see. Anything I point out to you that you haven't seen before doesn't count so don't try to scam me." The fifty cents is a real draw. I may live to regret this pecuniary bribe I think to myself. We tumble out of the truck and a friendly man sitting in a beach chair under a tree at the trail head rises in greeting. He reads over the information and directions at the bulletin board with us and tells us, "Have a good walk. Be sure to check for ticks on your way home. It's important." I notice that there are two other cars in the parking area besides my red truck and suspect that our greeter's main function is to be sure no more than the fifteen or so cars the area can accommodate try to crowd in.

Let's Walk, Lilly

The trail is fresh and manicured. Conor spots an oak, white oak, he explains by the rounded leaves. Then a black oak, pointy leaves. He's going strong. Corey spots poison ivy and they all echo his yell - a buck-fifty in a blink of an eye. "Don't get so close," I yell back. "It only takes seconds to get that ivy oil on your skin to start a rash." We pass under a marvelous spreading maple which I'm sure they could recognize but their eyes are everywhere else at the moment despite my stalling under the branches and coughing and pointing. Lee's been quiet. He's still getting used to his new friends although he keeps well up with them. "There's a squirrel," cries Conor. All I and the others see is a trembling and fluttering oak branch going away from us. "Are you sure that's a squirrel?" I ask Conor. "Sure, I saw it," he replies. It looked like the agitated branch of a squirrel's runway I think. "O.K. You all get the fifty cents."

"A humming bird," cries Lee. It's behind us and long gone when we turn around. Only fifty cents but that's a good find I think. The boys run and jostle each other along the increasingly down-hill path and we are suddenly almost at the shore. The short path to the right takes us to the look-out through the trees where we see a small shingle beach below and Vineyard Sound beyond. The water is gray today reflecting the partially overcast sky. The Elizabeth Islands are hazed out of sight, air sultry and hot. We are sweating even on the down-hill course. No more thought to nature except for the beckoning beach. We are there, shoes off, and into the water in a flash. "It's cold," they scream, as the Sound is always cold I think and refreshing too this hot day. The beach is 150 yards long, more or less, and nearly deserted, plenty of place for the four of us without being a bother to anyone else. All the time I am wondering how wise I am to be writing up this walk. Do I really want anyone else to find this idyllic place? I guess we Vineyarders are all contaminated with that gang-plank mentality: I've arrived; let's keep everybody else away from Paradise.

Lee is good at skimming stones. After one especially successful skim he holds up five fingers to show his glee. "The only thing wrong, Papa Russ," says Conor, "Is the stones you have to walk on to get off the beach into the water." Nothing comes free, I think. Conor is in the water more than the rest of us. I guess his feet get accustomed. When the time comes to go, the two brothers holler, "Can we go bare foot up the trail?" I weigh briefly the alternative as they already are packing up and putting shoes into back backs. "Sure, go ahead," the wise man says. Lee and I are more fastidious and struggle with our towels and wet sandy feet before donning sneakers and leading the group off the beach. As we approach two women on a blanket, I hear one say loud enough for me to hear, "He looks like the Pied Piper." I turn with a smile and think of the real pleasures of a grandparent on a hot day at the beach with three young boys.

At the top of the first and steepest climb we meet friends my age. They sit resting on a bench to the side of the trail looking a little dispiritedly at the increasing decline of the path. "I think I've reached my limit," the woman says. She looks tired. Her husband looks as if he might be disappointed not to go on. "What do you think, should I go all the way down?" she asks me directly. I don't have much hesitation in telling her I think her instincts are right. "Listen to your body," I say. That has become my mantra for most stresses in later life since my retirement. She looks relieved. The boys and I ascend the last incline and I notice that my friends are following.

Nine more cars have parked in the area since we came in. It hardly seemed that many people on the beach. We have had a good time and the kids pile into the truck. Later, before my boys return home with their parents, I try to cajole them into helping me with my piece for the Times. They seem at a loss. "Tell me what you remember, keep it simple. Just give me a few words I can use."

"O.K., Papa Russ", they say. In rapid fire order I jot down

verbatim the following: "Easy the walk, nice the beach, stony the beach." [Conor]; "Nice view from the cliff, leaf game, money earned, 9 bucks in all, barefoot return, red oak, poison ivy, black oak, beach grass, humming bird, squirrel, relieved to get to water, escape the heat, great kids because we are!" [Corey].

HOW TO GET THERE: Drive on State Road up-island just past Humphrey's Bakery and Deli in West Tisbury and turn right on North Road. Proceed 1.2 mile beyond Tea Lane and turn right at Land Bank logo, drive 0.5 mile to park. From the north end of Menemsha Cross Road drive down-island on North Road 0.3 mile just past Tabor House Road to the Land Bank sign on the left.

Trade Wind Fields Preserve   Mae Deary

Pecoy Point Preserve and Trade Wind Fields Preserve

Lilly and I bound up into the truck like a couple of kids. The weather change from hot and sultry to seventy-degree perfect has revitalized us both. We're off to Oak Bluffs on a double walk, two quite different and nearly adjacent preserves maintained by the Martha's Vineyard Land Bank. A friend called last week and asked if I'd ever walked to Pecoy Point. "Pecoy Point?" I asked, "Never heard of it." The new Land Bank Conservation Lands Map shows a small green spot, number 32, on the western shore of Major's Cove, part of Sengekontacket Pond behind State Beach. Near a number of homes, it is isolated and serene with a view across the pond to State Beach. Wind is up sharply from the northeast and I'm barely warm enough in a T-shirt. A five minute walk to the water along the trail takes us over salt meadow and marsh past a variety of wild flowers blooming in yellows, blues and orange. I recognize a yellow fox tail from the description at trail-head, even retrace my steps to make certain.

Coming along the shore we meet a young man carrying half a bucket of soft shells. He has a specially rigged plumber's helper staffed on an old broom handle, secured with a squeeze clamp. That's essential he tells me or else the rubber cup comes off about the third or fourth plunge. He's quit this morning ahead of his full bushel because his hands are numb from the cold water and feeling to the bottom for the clams brought toward the surface with his suction device. I'm sure he's carrying the clams home for a last Vineyard meal before returning to Manhattan where he tells me he teaches elementary school in Chinatown. He gets a shell fish license from Oak Bluffs every year for thirty-five bucks. I'd pay considerably more since I'm from Chilmark he tells me. There's no other activity on the pond this day. Cherry stones, little necks and oysters are resting undisturbed. We leave reluctantly to escape the wind and find the clammer standing against his parked car, hands warming on the broad sheet metal of the rear trunk.

This is a great place for "short" walkers to remove themselves from the bustle of the towns as respite on the edge of a peaceful pond. Botanists may recognize sand plain blue-eyed grass which blossoms in spring and early summer, eastern gamma grass, four to six feet tall and member of the corn family which blossoms in August, salt marsh and salt meadow cord grass, and spike grass. Bird watchers will spot northern harriers, American goldfinches and belted king fishers.

Back in the car park a boulder with neat bronze marker for the African-American Heritage Trail marks the vicinity of Pulpit Rock, formerly used by preachers to spread the word of the Lord. John Saunders, "born into enslavement in Virginia", was "pure African". He was transported here by Capt. T. Luce, "hidden by corn". His wife Priscilla was "half-white". They were both "zealous Christians." John, being an exhorter, preached to the people of color living at Farm Neck.

After a short drive toward Oak Bluffs, we're now having our first drink of water in the parking area at Trade Wind. There's no wind here and the temperature's rising, the sky clear. Lilly can't wait to get started again. As we start off along the long air strip, we read the sign cautioning us not to cross the strip for fear of the rare incoming plane. The land bank is preventing the air field from reverting to shrubs and trees. This seems a common theme on the Vineyard. Areas previously cleared by the toil of the early settlers have largely reverted to woodlands. Along the path four handsome and silky golden retrievers race across the strip in constant frolic. Many folks use this area for exercising their dogs. Lilly meekly greets two of them who bound around her. She lies supinely on the path until their curiosity is satisfied and their owner, a hundred yards away, gives out a barely heard command and they bound off toward her. Pitch pine woods border the air field. It is my least favorite Vineyard stand of trees. The trunks appear to have been painted with the same brush dipped in black tar. The outer bark scales upward. The trees look like good tinder. Here, they are dense but they don't seem to retard the growth of poison ivy which seems to creep out and burgeon everywhere it can reach the light.

The trail proceeds in a large square around the field. Emerald green to our left looks cool and refreshing through the trees as we walk along past the Farm Neck Golf Course. I could vote for another golf course if I were confronted with that choice today. As we proceed along I see that this preserve is sandwiched in among a lot of civilization: golf course, County Road and its traffic, many neatly kept homes and nearby a school. This is a treasure for everyone but especially for those nearby who have a quiet place to walk, to sit in the shade against a post, as I did half-way around the mile walk, or simply to unleash their dogs and let them run and run. Something in my memory tells me this area was once destined to be developed as golf course or hotel. Fortunately we have the old Trade Wind Fields under preservation for a long long time.

We come full square to the last hundred yards of the walk. The old hangars finally orient me. Somehow I kept looking for them in the wrong places. Suddenly I am back in the fifties, early in my years of practice on the Vineyard, a Saturday afternoon in the late fall, office hours in my old tweed suit getting baggier with each cleaning and a young boy with a belly ache. His father, one of my new friends, wants him to go immediately to the Mass. General in Boston. Med-evac as a term has not been coined. The only ambulances are the station wagons which each of the two undertakers maintain with a man-carried stretcher like the ones used on the battle field in WWII. Helicopters have not entered civilian life, certainly not on the Vineyard. Bob Love owns the Martha's Vineyard Shipyard and a license to fly a private plane. He occasionally helps transfer a sick patient to Boston. Afternoon is pressing on as Bob taxis his plane out of the hangar and we load the young man into the back where two seats have been removed. Taxiing down the grass strip is a bumpy jog but once airborne we sail along as smooth as silk. I sit up front with Bob and the trip goes without mishap except when we approach land again. The plane takes a lot of small jumps up and down. My stomach never seems to be in concert with the plane's gyrations. We land soon enough and deliver our patient to the waiting ambulance at Butler's Aviation.

Fall fog has been hanging around all evening. As we fly back toward the Vineyard, Mr. Love keeps looking over toward the horizon and seems a little uncomfortable. By the time we reach Vineyard Sound, just he and I now, the Vineyard is socked in. Can't possibly try to find the air strip in this soup, he tells me. We head over for New Bedford. A few minutes later he announces we've missed New Bedford. The fog and we are racing against each other. We'll just make Fall River, he thinks. The last bit of daylight is fast disappearing. Everything below is gray or black to my eyes. I tighten my belt. The Fall River field hits us from below directly to the solar plexus. "Oh, I'm so sorry," Robert says. I couldn't care less as long as we keep rolling along upright.

A taxi brings us into the city to look for a place to stay. A dingy hotel is the city's main attraction in these days. Bob in his jeans and dirty shirt and I in my baggy tweeds approach the check-in. Bob unrolls a deck of credit cards as long as my arm. I've used my last ten bucks paying the cab into town. He came away from chipping paint on his boat without any cash. The clerk eyes us with some suspicion. "Double bed or two singles," he says with a straight face. "Singles," Bob replies with a straight face and we're ready for a meal and a good night's sleep. Morning finds us still fogged in and we return to Woods Hole by taxi. I can't remember how we paid the cab. Bob made another trip to retrieve his plane.

I am sitting in my truck with good pal, Lilly, remembering how well the young patient made out in Boston, how grateful his father and mother were, how grateful I was that Bob Love had a plane and we beat the fog and what a nice day it has been here in Oak Bluffs today.

[Author's Note: I have always been puzzled by the name Trade Wind Fields. In my mind Trade Winds Fields is intuitively correct. I found the latter current in "Martha's Vineyard – Detailed Road Map," published by Edward L. Thomas, 1999. Knowing Mr. Thomas as a scholarly fellow I assumed he might have something and I called James Lengyel at the land bank and heard an interesting story. Mr. Lengyel had a call from Ms. Carolyn Cullen before she died who told him that when she bought the small airport in Oak Bluffs she named it "Trade Wind Airport." She was quite emphatic Lengyel said that she wanted "Trade Wind" to remain after it was taken over by the land bank. Since the land bank no longer was running an airport, they substituted "Fields" in the name and so it stands.]

HOW TO GET THERE: Pecoy Pt.: From Edgartown, proceed toward Vineyard Haven 3.2 mi on Edgartown-Vineyard Haven Road., then right on County Road toward Oak Bluffs. (From the blinker light, County Road is 1.1 miles toward Edgartown on the left). Drive on County 0.9 mile to Pulpit Rock Road (entrance to Water View Farms opposite Meadow

View Farms), turn right, go 0.2 mi and bear right at Pecoy Pt. sign, another 0.3 mi to parking on right. Or, from Oak Bluffs Fire Station at corner of County/Wing/Barnes Roads, go 2.3 mi to Pulpit Rock Rd, turn left, follow as above.

Trade Wind Fields: From Edgartown or blinker light, turn off Edg-VH Road to County Road, go 2.0 mi to Farm Neck Road on right. Continue on County Road. to stop sign, turn right at Wing Road (Oak Bluffs Fire Station across street on right). Turn right again at first street on right (Pheasant Lane), turn left at the end, then right and follow long wooden rail to park on left.

SUMMER

Long Point   Ralph Stewart

Long Point in Summer

This third week in August - the time of Oak Bluffs' Illumination, West Tisbury's Agricultural Fair, and peak numbers of our summer friends on the highways and byways - is time for a special destination for even the most jaded of us. My choice is Long Point Wildlife Refuge on the West Tisbury south shore, owned and managed since 1979 by the oldest conservation group in the country, The Trustees of Reservations. My last tour was in mid-winter of 2000 when the wind blasted Rafe Teller and me almost to freezing and roared so loudly over the dunes from the sea we could scarcely hear each other speak. Today provides a sharp contrast.

The weather has been in the 80s and the sun bright since a brief but powerful downpour a week ago. My neighbors and I start early to be sure we snag one of the 120 parking spots at the reservation. Tim, his daughter, Emma, and son, Lee, from Wisconsin, Tim's friend Bernie from Vermont and I set out for Waldron's Bottom Road opposite the airport on West Tisbury Road. We're loaded with bottled water, snacks, sunscreen and towels. Everyone wears a swim suit in anticipation of a swim. My trustee membership card helps defray the modest cost of parking and admission and the khaki-clad attendants are helpful in pointing out the way to the inland pond beach and the trails beyond. "The water is tested daily, nice and clean!"

If you haven't ventured on one of the south shore beaches available to the public you haven't really seen a breath-taking beach like this one. It stretches as far as you can see in either direction, unobstructed by vegetation, rocks, or buildings anywhere in view. On one side there is nothing but the sea running all the distance to Spain and on the other, only pristine dunes. Few people have gathered at this hour and we proceed west to the first cut in the dunes back toward land to approach the smaller sheltered beach at the end of Long Cove. Young families are already spreading blankets, planting umbrellas and ministering to a varied age group of young from infants in sacks to 12 and 14 year olds helping their elders establish a spot for the day.

Emma, 14, is the first into the water with a graceful plunge and immediately looks back to be sure we've all noticed. Lee, 11, is more guarded and takes his time, eventually spending most of the time submerged, all but his head which stays amazingly dry for the whole time. We adults take the lazy way out and sit on the towels watching and enjoying the chance to relax. Tim and Bernie have been friends since the University of Illinois School of Architecture. They spent a winter in Paris as part of a five year program. "Here I am," Tim says with an expression of disbelief. "I'm sitting on a bench in view of the palace at Versailles and saying to myself, 'What's a kid from the mid-west doing in the middle of France?'" Bernie laughs knowing exactly how Tim was feeling. Each acknowledges that they took little time finding out just why they were there. The inevitable topic of winter weather in Vermont prompts Bernie to say that they had scarcely a day below zero last season. A bit of uncommon good luck I think.

After most of an hour the kids come back for their towels and begin munching on Multi-Grain bars or Pop-Tarts. We haven't had much walking today and Tim spurs us on even without a swim. Down the outside beach, Emma kneels in the sand at water's edge. "Look at the pig crab," she cries. "Dad used to dig a big hole at the water line and let it fill with water. Then we'd scoop up those little crabs and throw them into the pool. The first one that buried itself into the sand would win. They looked like little pigs and that's how we named them." Emma is describing sand bugs or mole crabs.

A little farther along the outer beach we find another cut which takes us up onto the great grassy plain, under restoration by the Trustees. Waste-high huckleberry and other greens and remnants of oaks rise up out of the ashes of a recent burn or massive cutting. Ten or twelve birds frantically circle a lone bird house propped on a pole. Either an interesting resident within beckons or the multitude is vying for the same abode. We're soon attracted to hundreds of similar birds, mostly black, many with light undersides and all with the shape and flying patterns of swallows, large swallows. Purple martins they must be. Like soldiers at dress parade, they line up on the scrub all facing the wind and the sea. As we pass they rise in flight only to settle down a little farther on in the same pattern. Off to the east is a clump of rose blossoms, waving in the considerable breeze. They must be either late blooming beach rose or rose of Sharon.

We turn off to our right after conferring with a ranger coming down from the only building in view at the edge of the woods ahead. Soon we can see the effects of one of the recent prescribed burns to encourage the restoration of indigenous plants. The trunks of the oaks are blackened to a height of eight or ten feet, yet the upper branches with buds seem to be alive. We compare opposite sides of the path. On the left the underbrush is dense and four to six feet high. On the right there is nothing but ankle deep grass and early regrowth. In the short distance through the trees the silvery water of Long Cove glistens. The breeze we felt on the grassy plain has deserted us here in the sheltered woods and the air is hot and steamy without it. I look back and Lee is trailing the group munching on his second Pop-Tart. "Lee, once the energy of that tart reaches your muscles, you'll take over the lead." I tease him a little but get no response. Only a few minutes later I see him way out in front without effort it seems.

Our trail crosses the main sandy road back to the winter parking area and maintenance buildings. We follow the Middle Cove Trail. Once again I see this sheltered inlet, lined with uniform oaks on the far bank and tranquil mirror-like water in the foreground. What's missing is the swan from my last wintry visit. We return to the sandy road and head back for the beach. "Look at this," exclaims Lee. We all stand around him while he watches something moving too fast or too distantly for any of us to see. "There, close to the road." he says. A tiny reddish insect skimmers by and out of sight into the brush at the roadside. How did he ever spot it I ask myself? Once again he stops our march. "A caterpillar," he shouts. We all lean over to see a very small green caterpillar, nearly indistinguishable from the road bed, making its torturous way along a rut. "He won't have a long journey if a car comes along," his father says. Several times I see Lee pointing out something to his father in the brush or at a tree.

We retrace our steps on the beach heading for the parking area. Now there are legions of beach-goers with blankets and umbrellas, radios and kids. Some venturous souls are in the surf, not very high today but nevertheless not for sissies. A deeply tanned middle aged man stands looking out to the ocean and gesturing with his arm as if to warn a woman in knee deep water twenty feet away not to venture any farther out. She doesn't respond. As we approach the man, we can see he is holding a cell phone to his ear and gesticulating to punctuate his conversation, or perhaps to drive it, not, as we thought, trying to retrieve his wife from danger. He is still talking and gesticulating as we reach our path to leave the beach. "I imagine he's brought his business to the shore today," I say to Tim and Bernie. We all smile and say no more.

This time the parking lot is nearly full and cars are still arriving. I'm glad we came early. Emma is already a little pink despite her sun screen. Its time for lunch at home. As we drive along the airport road again I can't keep out of mind two quite different images - one, of Lee and Emma discovering intricate or hidden gems of the environment, and the second, the cell phone user on the beach who as yet seems not to have discovered the Vineyard.

HOW TO GET THERE: Mid June thru Mid September: Drive 0.3 miles past the Dukes County Airport toward W. Tisbury, turn left on Waldron's Bottom Road. Follow 1.3 mi, turn left on Watcha Road (Path), then quickly right on Hughe's Thumb Road for 1.2 miles to summer parking. Mid September thru mid June: Drive 1.1 mile past the airport toward W. Tisbury, turn left on Deep Bottom Road and follow for 1.5 miles always taking left forks. Turn right on Thumb Point Road and follow 1.3 miles to off-season parking.

View from Menemsha Hills

Kenneth Vincent

Discovery Walk at Menemsha Hills Reservation

On a morning in July, Andrew Kendall, recently appointed Executive Director of The Trustees of Reservations, meets about twenty-five hikers at the parking area for Menemsha Hills Reservation to get acquainted with the Vineyard. His trip is part of a state-wide series of visits from Gloucester in the east to Williamstown in the west and back to the southeast and the Island. He will have visited nine preserves and opened a new one at Slocum's River Preserve in Dartmouth.

A native of Massachusetts and a graduate of Amherst College and the Harvard Business School, Andy lives with his wife Emilie and son Oliver in Newton. He speaks enthusiastically about his recent five-year experience in Boston working with Massachusetts Audubon Society to create a nature preserve, trails and 500 family garden plots on the grounds of the now defunct Boston State Hospital. Long abandoned and neglected, the hospital was razed by the state following which the Audubon Society obtained 68 acres of the hospital grounds, part of Boston's largest swath of undeveloped land which is bordered by Mattapan, Dorchester, Roxbury, Jamaica Plain and Hyde Park.

Mr. Kendall's move from The Audubon Society to the Trustees seems fortuitous. The Trustees of Reservations, originated in 1891 by Charles Eliot who was a protégé of Frederick Law Olmsted, is the oldest private conservation organization in the country with over 80 reservations in Massachusetts. According to the Trustees introductory statement, the new director comes to his position with a passion for "their mission of saving special places for people's enjoyment and benefit and

brings to the job an extraordinary blend of experience in conservation, advocacy, business management, collaboration and
fund raising."

As his first official visit to the Island, the new Trustees
Director has chosen one of my favorite Island places. Menemsha
Hills Reservation is 211 acres of woodland, heath, sand cliff,
stony beach, and marshland. Three other Vineyard preserves
are maintained by the Trustees: Long Point Wildlife Refuge in
West Tisbury, Wasque Reservation and Mytoi Garden, both on
Chappaquiddick, all impressive and unique in their own right.
The day is warm and clear. Coffee and doughnuts are on hand
while the group gathers and Mr. Kendall introduces himself to
everyone. Two reporters snap photographs and there is an air of
anticipation for a special walk this morning. Naturalist Suzan
Bellingcampi directs the tour with help from Chris Kennedy,
Islands Regional Director of the Trustees' properties, Chris
Egan, Refuge Manager for up-island, and Sonya Beausoliel,
ranger.

At a pretty good pace Ms. Bellingcampi leads on into the
shaded oak woods pointing out "discoveries" on the way. "We
had a project among the school children to find vernal pools on
the property," she relates. "These are very special places and
require identification of certain animal forms within them to
become certified by the state as true vernal pools. There is only
one on the property and our kids found it. Wetlands are identified by the plant life sustained there, vernal pools by the animal
life." As she points out a depression beyond some fairly dense
shrubs, she tells how the children scooped the tiny life forms
from the pool with nets. It would be hard going to reach it I
think. I assume the pools are called vernal because they usually
fill with water in springtime and may go dry by summer.

We see examples of kettle holes, large depressions left by
giant chunks of ice which rested in the sand and rocky debris of

the last glacier. After the ice melted an empty hole remained in the midst of small rocks and sand. Suzan cautions that the landscape has also been altered by human use and one can't always be sure that some of the large holes one finds here may not have been caused by the removal of boulders for the Oak Bluffs jetty many years ago. She points to stone walls and reminds us that a hundred years ago all this land was bare of trees and shrubbery from the constant grazing of sheep. My walking companion, Alden Besse adds, "The walls were probably built as much to clear the land as to confine the sheep."

We ascend a modest hill to an opening in the trees and a breathtaking view of the entire western extremity of the Vineyard from Noman's Land on the south to Aquinnah on the west to the Elizabeths on the north: Cutty Hunk, Nashawena, Pasque and Naushon. In the foreground are Menemsha Pond and its village and harbor. In back of us at the apex of the hill is a pile of stone, placed there by competitive Prospect Hill residents in an effort to claim thereafter the highest point on the Island, surpassing the 311 feet of Peaked Hill to the south.

Back in the woodlands, Suzan points out a wild cherry, identified by the unique fungus growing on its leaves. The delicate erect fungus bodies, each on a stem mounted by an elongated seed-like structure, overall barely a quarter inch in height, sit along the central vein of a leaf. I think they resemble three or four surfers standing along one board. On another bush an unusual caterpillar has laid its eggs on the upper surface of a long leaf, then curled the leaf up and in, sealing all joined margins to make an air-tight cocoon. Yellow heather, now past bloom, and bearberry line the path with assorted fern as we descend on the lower trail to a tall beetle bung grove. Suzan asks us if we know what this island term for the tupelo or sour gum tree means. I have forgotten and she fortunately doesn't single me out for the answer: beetle from the old English betel or mallet; bung from the middle Dutch bonghe or stopper. Old-time whalers found the wood of these trees tough and resilient for use both as the bung for the whale oil kegs and as the mallet to hammer the bung into the bunghole of the barrel.

Reluctantly we press on from the grove of tupelos. The shade and leafless branches underneath as we leave contrast with the bright green canopy we see from a distant rise in the trail looking back. At the top of the rise we head to the great sand cliff where a wood platform projects us to the edge for an unobstructed view of Naushon and Woods Hole across Vineyard Sound. Down the beach to the east a thin jagged remnant of red brick chimney juts up from the encroaching jungle of green. It once exhausted the kiln furnaces which fired the bricks of the Boston Brick and Tile Company, later the Chilmark Brick Company. Suzan produces an old photo of a Chilmark hillside in this same locale but different from the densely treed vista we see here today. Her picture, circa 1900, shows an unbelievably bare and rocky landscape. It must have been taken at a time when the brick works had leveled the surrounding countryside of burnable wood and had begun to use more expensive coal, understandably one of the causes of the yard's demise.

As we catch our breath and prepare for the hike back to the trail-head, Suzan tells a little of the plans for the Trustees continued research and planned publications to document the ecology and history of their sites. Already a large pamphlet outlining the "History of Land Use at Long Point" is available from Trustees headquarters, the Vineyard Historical Society and possibly the town libraries. Another publication is planned for similar studies on Wasque Preserve. Our trek back, in the hotter part of the morning, is at a slower pace and relaxed. A woman hiker describes a kettle hole pond we seem to have missed on the way in. "Perhaps it's on the Harris loop, an alternate route to and from our starting point, as we return," she says. Alden and

I, trudging along beside her, can't remember a body of water along either arm of the Harris loop. I'm sure it's there," she insists. Sure enough, we pass her tiny pond now almost hidden by the tall trail-side growth of blueberry and further obscured by a complete surface of gray pollen. Otherwise the tiny pond is mirror-like under the protection of tall oaks.

Already more hikers are approaching onto the trail as we return to the parking area. We have had a special treat today, not only visiting or revisiting one of the Vineyard's premier trails but accompanied by our naturalist-extraordinaire, Suzan, and her new boss of the domain. We shake hands again with our hosts and wish Director Andrew Kendall imagination and resourcefulness in his work for The Trustees.

HOW TO GET THERE: Drive on the North Road to Chilmark and 0.6 mile past Tabor House Road on the right you will find the entrance marked with the Trustees logo. Turn in and park at the area provided at the top of the hill.

A Walk with an Angel

Some days are not suited for long walks or serious walks on preservation trails, historical trails, or any particularly defined trail. This day is one of those for reasons not exactly clear at the outset. For one thing the weather is oppressive, muggy with promise of showers later. For another, my inner walking spirit is not answering the various messages I send it about the approaching deadline for my article. But undoubtedly the overwhelming reason that this day is not propitious is the telephone call at nine-fifteen this morning from Gabriella's mother that she would like Gramma and Grampy to baby-sit for the morning.

Like a gum drop that has sat in its dish too long during a humid spell in August, I tend to get soft and mushy when Gabriella calls or, in this case, when her mother, Pam, my daughter-in-law, calls for her. Normally I can resist favors others ask of me if I am intent on something else, in this case a serious walk. Not when Gabby is involved. No sir, within ten minutes I am shaved, brushed and dressed, headed in the pick-up for down-island with spirits lifted and a hum in my throat of a very happy tune.

Gabriella is no ordinary run-of-the-mill girl. At four she is a blond princess, twinkly-eyed, given to a certain vampishness which melts my brain into something just short of dementia. "Hello, Grampy," she greets me in her driveway as I'm adjusting the child seat to be sure we have a safe journey back to Menemsha. The hairs on the back of my neck stir just enough to let me know I am once again under her spell. Before Gabriella can ask, "Do you want some of my peanut butter cup?," I've lifted her in the air and brought her down into the biggest bear hug she's had all day although it's only 9:45 am at this juncture. "Ooh, Grampy, you're squeezing me," she coos and of course I release her immediately and start loading the bags of accessories onto the floor in front of her seat for her morning stay at Gramma's house. Fully ensconced we say a cheery good-bye to her mother and head for the open road. A stop at the auto parts store in Vineyard Haven finishes serious work for the day. Gabriella squeezes in beside me as I negotiate the purchase of windshield wipers. She takes in everybody at the busy counter with wide eyes and a shy look from around the back of my legs. Each time we cross the parking lot she says, "I always hold your hand when we cross the street, Grampy." Someone has taught her well. Thank goodness the serious stuff is left to others.

By the time we head down hill toward the Menemsha Store for the morning Globe, we have identified trucks, motorcycles, bikers too close to the yellow line, and an assortment of way stations which she nods at as I recite their names and locations. Toward the end of the car ride her gaze fixes on the passing road-side as if she is about to fall asleep. It's a good thing her grandmother isn't here to chide me for running a veritable travelogue while we are simply driving from one place to the other. "Would you like to come inside the store with me?" She nods enthusiastically, grasping my hand firmly in hers, and we cross the congested little road to the store where we greet Kevin wrestling a case of ice cubes into his freezer. Globe in hand we leave without Gabriella's asking for a thing. Perhaps I've made the trip too hastily for her to notice the display of nickel and dime candies right inside the front door or the freezer full of ice cream bars and Eskimo pies.

The Galley next door is closed this early in the morning so there's no way to buy her ice cream here and we saunter up the roadway past the fishing shacks and the back porch of the Galley. "Gabriella, look at all the cormorants on the roof of the Coast Guard shed." The large black birds cluster there in the filtered sun light. "They don't have natural oil to keep their wings dry," I say. I'm now in what Gramma would call my tutorial mood. "Ooh, look at all the poop," Gabby says and wrinkles up her nose. True enough, the dark roof is splattered with at least fifty pounds of white droppings, characteristic of a bird's perch. It is a mess I have to admit and Gabriella knows what is important to take from one of my little snippets of info-speak. She's an excellent observer and says exactly what's on her mind.

"Look at all that gook in the water," she comments with a little squeal. Old weed, flotsam and foam of a peculiar yellow-gray quality are trapped in a large dead-end eddy inside the jetty against the bulkhead, not a pretty sight. Fortunately it doesn't smell. Then she spies a cormorant, this time swimming in the channel close to the dock where we stand. "Watch, now," the professor says. "He'll dive in a minute to catch some breakfast." Of course I'm right and down he goes much to Gabriella's delight. She looks intently for him to re-emerge and jumps up and down as he does. "Let's go home, Grampy. I want to see Lilly, and Gramma." The springer will be ecstatic to see her and Gramma is probably wondering where we have been. Kids' attention spans are limited and fortunately I'm trained to understand and respect that within certain limits.

"We're on the bumpy road now," she says. "Flander's Lane it's called," I say. "Named after the Flanders who own the big farm house over there on the right. "Is this your lane?" she asks. "Well, not exactly. Our lane is at the end. See if you can tell when we get there." Flander's Lane is not the smoothest road on the island or the worst but it takes only five or six minutes before we reach the last turn at Marjo's Way leading to our house at the end. "Here it is," she says.

After Gramma has administered her own mother bear hug and Lilly, the springer spaniel, has lapped her face and midriff and knees a dozen times, Gramma says, "Go on up to the garden and see if you can find me some tomatoes and cucumbers, a little parsley and basil." Gabriella is off at a run with her grandfather following. "I see some red ones," she cries as she tries to manhandle a ripe tomato from its tough vine attachment. I ease the fruit free and she places it carefully in the basket. "There's another ... and another." She is now a garden enthusiast. "Don't forget the cucumber," I admonish. We have already had a lesson in vegetables at Kevin's store in Menemsha. She recognizes them on the ground shaded by their big leaves. She is soon expert at wrestling them from the vines and we have a full basket. The carrot row is just ahead and I loosen several of the big ones and show her how to pull them out of the ground. "This is a really long one," she says, brushing off the dirt and arranging it alongside the cukes. "Now for the parsley and basil and we're done," I say and we close the gate behind us and return to the house.

It's time for the women to have their time and I retire to my desk with the sound of "women's voices" burbling in the background. I wonder if I will ever return to serious walks or have I found that this may be the most rewarding one I've ever taken?

HOW TO GET THERE: Find one of your favorite little people to invite on a personal tour of a familiar haunt. Drive or walk but not too far and spend some uncluttered moments, hours, or the day just having fun. Details will fall into place.

FALL

By mid-September Vineyard life has slowed. The pulse in
your head runs rapidly for so long on the run, racing against
time and then palpably slows to a trot, then a walk and there is
relief. We'd forgotten how fast we'd been traveling. Traffic has
been thinning since late August, ever so little at first, and then
one day along State Road toward Vineyard Haven we ask ourselves with shock, "Where have all the people gone?" This is the
season when we native Vineyarders take deep breaths every
morning feeling the world has returned to its usual place. It's a
selfish notion, inescapable really, for those of us who live here
year-round. Thoughts turn to bass and the big blues, empty
beaches just for the taking, water clear and cool but warm
enough for a swim well toward October. The land takes on a
golden hue and birds fly everywhere. Cronig's and the A&P are
more navigable, prices seem to have fallen off a little, and
there's more time to chat with friends at the post office and
while pumping gas at Texaco.

Fall is the best time of year, too bad for summer visitors who
must return to school and work and leave just when everything
turns to perfection. Certainly change is everywhere, as if there
is a new beginning, yet when we walk in the woods the evidence
is of ending – leaves falling, ferns turning brown and wilted, the
sour smell of vegetation turning back to earth and the long Vees
of ducks, glimpsed through bare-boughed trees and scurrying
south before the icy winds of winter catch them unawares. On a
dry day the leaves under foot crackle and crunch broadcasting
your steps far and wide. On a wet damp day the leaves under
foot silence your steps and the impulse of stepping is transmit-

ted through to your bones and no where else. Days shorten and the evening chill grows sharp. Suddenly at Halloween clocks are peremptorily turned back creating blinding sunlight in your waking eyes and dark cold afternoons when outside work and play cease too early.

Soon the dividend of Indian summer also finishes and the last of November, gray and slanted with clouds over a thin cold sunset, rings out this season as we stack our firewood and make the last fixes on homes for winter.

Brine's Pond Preserve   Ralph Stewart

Brine's Pond Preserve
and Chappy Five Corners Preserve

With Hurricane Floyd bearing down on Florida later this week and then who knows where, I call Curry Jones on Chappy and arrange to meet him on his end of the ferry at 9 am, a Monday, clear and invigorating for this early in September. I suspect that Floyd, in at least some indirect way, has a hand in the muggy weather which has preceded this surprisingly light day. Brine's Pond Preserve and Chappy Five Corners Preserve, two of the Martha's Vineyard Commission Land Bank's preserves are near each other on Chappaquiddick. I am a relative stranger there, therefore the call to Curry to accompany me in foreign territory. He and wife Peggy have lived there several years since retirement. Being an outdoor type he will be a good guide. I meet them as appointed along with a new traveling companion, Ginger. She's a large senior Labrador whose color is a mix of black and a deep honey sheen, thus, I suspect, the name. Peggy drops us off at the short road into the Chappaquiddick Community Center where the Brine's Pond trail begins. The center itself is an impressive building, very busy in summer, Curry says, but also staging regular activities all year long.

We plan our course at the small map to start. Red to green to yellow trails will take us to a V-cornered turn of the yellow trail at the western extremity of the preserve. The early morning clarity and stillness of Brine's Pond at the outset of our walk makes talking an intrusion for a time. The grass along the path is heavy with dew and the new season almost upon us is just barely seen in the turning and falling of a few of the leaves. "This is a great trail," Curry says finally. He's quick to say that years before the land bank existed he and Peggy had walked here on old trails. "You'll have to visit Poucha Pond over near our place," he continues. "I helped cut most of those trails well before the land bank acquired it for a preserve." Except for the pond shining in sun and a large field being developed by the land bank, this area is entirely woodland. The paths are broad and mostly covered with soft pine needles. "Great trail," Curry murmurs again.

Ginger lumbers along taking little notice of us. She's a quieter walker than my old standby, Lilly, less snorting down among the undergrowth somehow. We come to a sharp turn in the yellow trail now and find a small hand painted map with directions to proceed up to Sampson's Hill and take the left hand Sampson Hill Road. From there Chappy Five Corners is a half mile distant. "I remember when that house was built," Curry says as we proceed up a narrow foot path squeezed between overhanging shrubs and an occasional large truant flag of poison ivy. Nearby on the opposite side two people sit secluded on an open porch above us. We can hear the murmur of conversation. Another house almost immediately ahead on the right looms up. "This has changed since I was last here," Curry observes. A man tinkering with his car parked in the drive confirms that the road to the right goes back down to the Chappaquiddick Road where Peggy left us. We follow the previous directions to go to the left. Somehow I don't quite trust Curry's intuition we're on the right path. Even he seems a little uncertain because of the new houses and their separate driveways crossing the area. We're on an old dirt road with grassy median, easy on foot. I hang back, now disoriented by looking at the two small maps in the guide book. "I have to know how to describe this," I tell my companion. "We'd better go back and have another look at that map." Sure enough, the map clearly shows all the details we need - the apex of the yellow trail pointing us to the narrow up-hill path, the directions to go up the hill and take the road to the left. "The devil's always in the details," I say. Curry refrains from saying I told you so. If I had looked more carefully, the directions would have been obvious enough. Up we trail again past the folks on their porch for the third time. "They'll wonder what we're doing," Curry laughs. "Probably think we're mapping out a new bus route for the VTA," I say with a straight face.

Sampson's Hill is just ahead, all 94 feet of it above sea level, marked by a brass plate on a boulder. Here existed a semaphore station dating from very early in the 19th century, used to relay word of the arrival of a new cargo of whale oil at Nantucket by signals from Nantucket via Nonamessett Island, thence to West Chop and Woods Hole. This is the highest spot on Chappy.

The half mile down the road to Five Corners is a comfortable ramble in quiet woods. We take the silver trail to the right after turning in by the land bank sign for Five Corners and skirt a large swamp in the middle of the preserve. It is out of view because of thick growth of bushes and trees. Two or three houses nestle mostly out of sight. A single truck passes ahead of us into a private drive. Curry knows who lives in each house and at the end of every dirt road branching off. "I'll have to bring Peggy out soon for more walks," Curry says. Another trail branch turns left over the swamp but Ginger seems to be tiring and we've had a good bit of exercise ourselves. We leave crossing the swamp to another time and emerge into the trail head, by reverse in effect, and a parking area. Curry has planned well because we are only ten minutes away from his house on Wasque Road, one of the contributions to the five corners along with Chappaquiddick Road which enters a broad-curved turn here, Litchfield Road and another, unnamed. The unscreened sun along the tarmac is hotter by degrees than when we started and Ginger, senior as she is, is tired. She stops in the middle of her own driveway and lies down. She's saying she's home, I'll go no farther. Her legs shake a little as she lies down. Then I think she remembers her water dish in the kitchen and rises to make a passably good appearance at the back door for Peggy.

HOW TO GET THERE: Brine's Pond Preserve: Park at the Chappaquiddick Community Center on the right, 1.7 mi from ferry slip on Chappaquiddick Road. Total walk about 1.0 mile. Chappy Five Corner's: Park on right side of Chappaquiddick Road. 3.3 mi from ferry slip. Total walk about 0.5 mi. If you want to take both areas in the same walk, follow directions at the V-apex of the yellow trail in Brine's Pond Preserve to the Sampson Hill Road and continue to Chappy Five Corners. Unless someone meets you at the end of that trail with a car, the walk back to the Brine's Pond trail head along Chappaquiddick Road is another 1.6 miles. Total combined walk about 3.6 mi.

FALL

Poucha Pond   Stephen Warriner

Poucha Pond Reservation

Poucha Pond has one of those Vineyard names probably derived from the Native- American which is not pronounced as it looks in print, not at least by knowledgeable Chappy residents like my guide, Curry Jones. I ask him to walk with me to POWTCHA POND. As usual he is enthusiastic but later in our conversation he inserts, a little obviously I think, that he'll see me at POHTCHA POND on Friday morning. I know that he's correct but somehow, not speaking Chappaquidick-ese very often in everyday life, I've forgotten. From now on it's Poucha with an "oh" instead of an "ow" in the middle. The area in question is a 99 acre preserve owned and managed by Martha's Vineyard Land Bank. Curry leaves his lab, Ginger, behind today. He tells me, "A hunter carrying a bird rifle told me last week anyone who runs his dog in the woods these days of hunting ought to have his head examined." I begin to feel a little self conscious wearing my bright orange L.L. Bean jacket as I drive through Edgartown to the Chappy ferry. I imagine heads and eyes turning as I pass. When I see Curry in his own orange jacket I know I am properly attired. We set out just a stone's throw from his own back door off the Chappaquiddick Road a little past Chappy Five Corners. A chill in the air tells us it is November but altogether pleasant and windless. New red placards nailed to the tree near the trail-head warn walkers to be dressed in orange; it is hunting season. We are wise in leaving Ginger behind and to be dressed as we are. In fact, since a local housewife found an arrow nearly on her back doorstep a week ago, there are new signs posting the 500 foot hunting limit from occupied buildings.

We start on the red trail through pitch pine woodlands where poison ivy grows abundantly under and about these black-barked scaly pines. Soon we come to oaks arching overhead although many of their leaves are now falling to ground and the view through the woods is lengthening as fall progresses. Curry has cut most of these trails himself in years past before the land was conveyed to the land bank. He thinks the time may have been twenty years before. Neither one of us, it turns out, is accurate about gauging times distant for events in our lives. Everything seems to have happened just yesterday. Curry again takes proprietary note of one of his small branching trails which we bypass.

The red trail leads to the blue and we find ourselves out of the woods with the pond in the distance. The focal point of Poucha Pond is the marsh abutting it. As we step out of the bushes at woods edge the marsh opens up ahead and to the sides. Beyond the marsh are the dunes of East Beach. Small elevations of wooded and scrubby "land islands" of high ground interrupt the flat plane of grass. Distance from car tires humming on pavement and ocean surf rolling on shore imposes a quiet on this whole area. Even our voices are lowered I think and we stand gazing over the tan gently waving salt meadow grass and the occasional marsh hawk gliding overhead.

The water is low today across the marsh; we can stay dry walking the grassy causeway across the center of the marsh to the first island ahead. Curry says that other days we might need water-proof shoes or boots. We see the difference in growth from the uniform meadow grass over most of the area and the encroaching species which grow near the causeway where the salt water is less intrusive. In fact, two species of Spartina (S.) grass dominate most marshes. S. alterniflora or tall cord grass grows in proximity to the leading edge of a marsh, closest to the ocean salt water. S. patens or salt meadow grass, the silkier shorter grass we see here, grows in the higher portions of the marsh where the salt is less concentrated yet the tides flood the area at intervals. The development of these grasses represents an evolutionary adjustment to their environment with internal systems to regulate the concentration of salt, the evaporation and absorption of water and the exchange of carbon dioxide and oxygen. I see clouds of small white fuzzy growths on top of green bushes at marsh edge. They are miniature powder puffs of short white hairs close to the crotches of leaf and stem. Later at home I will triumphantly identify these as swamp myrtle or "consumption weed" with burst seed pods.

We talk about the old times when farming was the order of the day here and on most of the Vineyard. Early settlers found these marshes an abundant source of ready grown hay. Virgin marshes were uniform and clean, free from weeds and invasive species. The hay could be had for the cutting without laborious clearing of trees and rocks. Marshes of the sort that we see at Poucha could be harvested with the ordinary tools or machinery needed for cutting and carting away. If the marsh was too wet and soft for carting, the hay was piled on top of poles like the frame of a battlefield stretcher for the wounded. The hay then was carried to a platform of poles set into the marsh. Of course, at times of high tides or storm flooding, the stacks might float away and have to be retrieved by the farmer. There are stories of greedy farmers who would pursue the floating haycocks belonging to a neighbor and stick them with a pole marking them as their own. Later when the marsh was frozen, a horse and wagon could venture out to retrieve the stacked hay. In modern times, salt meadow hay is not used so much for fodder as it is for healthy weed-free garden mulch.

"Life and Death of the Salt Marsh" by John and Mildred Teale, from which much of the information above is derived, is an almost lyrical account of the marshes as we see them along the whole of the northeast coast. Writing thirty years ago, the Teals describe the birth of the marsh from the early invasion of the great glaciers, their retreat, and colonization by early soil, plant growth, insects, fish and fowl and game. The marshes were and are an invaluable part of our ecosystem, not only for their beauty but for their nurturing of plant life, shell fish and other fish, a source for food and nesting of many birds and animal life. I wonder when I trespass on a marsh what gives it the springy feel without necessarily my feet becoming immersed in water which flows just below. As succeeding seasons of meadow grass lie unharvested, they fall under the new growth of the next summer and form a resilient base under which the water lies and on top of which the new grass waves in the breeze. The Teals also recount the death of a marsh as the result of uninformed land use management, including ditching and extensive spraying with DDT, by succeeding generations of settlers. The saddest picture in their book is a drawing of a marsh at the edge of a seacoast city being filled with garbage and trash from the burgeoning community beyond. We know, from standing at the edge of Poucha Pond, that this marsh looks to last well beyond our times in ever improving condition.

Passing through the first land island's scrubby growth, almost before I realize it, we pass over another causeway, barely discernible as a four foot wide elevation across the marsh, to the second island. At its far edge we encounter more marsh and, beyond to the right, the dunes of East Beach and Wasque. A mood of tranquility prevails. We follow another short trail through woods on our left to the pond again and look north to the Dike Bridge and beginning of Cape Pogue Pond. We reluctantly turn away from the scene to complete our loop around the yellow trail. Much of the surrounding woodlands on private property features inviting and well manicured trails. Back at Peggy Jones's kitchen table for coffee and almond flavored toast strips, I recall Curry's subtle lesson: "Poucha with an "Oh!" not an "Ow!"

HOW TO GET THERE: Take the Chappaquiddick ferry in Edgartown, drive 3.8 miles on Chappaquiddick Road and turn in to left to park at trail head.

Sheriff's Meadow

Ralph Stewart

Sheriff's Meadow Sanctuary

I leave Menemsha early morning in my pick-up and head down-Island for a walk around Sheriff's Meadow in Edgartown. My thoughts are full of the magical adventures in J.K. Rowling's "Harry Potter and The Sorcerer's Stone". It may not be seemly to admit reading such a children's book but nevertheless I am under its spell. Absorbed as I am, I hardly notice two loud thumps in the back of the truck as I pass through the center of West Tisbury. Seeing nothing in my rear view mirror I continue on and reach Edgartown where I park in the town lot back of the school. Leaving the truck I nearly jump out of my skin to see two passengers disembarking from the back. "When did you get into my truck?" I exclaimed. I was so surprised I barely remembered why I had come to Edgartown in the first place. Then I recalled the thumps while passing the church in West Tisbury. "How did you get in there? You must have flown down from the steeple."

"Never mind that," says the first to step toward me, a young woman under twenty whom I now recognized as Hermione, Harry Potter's school chum from Hogwarts School of Witchcraft and Wizardry. The young man with glasses is Harry himself. "Never mind how we got here," they say in unison. "The point is we're here and we are going with you on your walk." By now we have started and are abreast of Cannon Ball Park on the Main Street side. A portly man in waist coat and florid tie stands straight upon a soap box near the cannon balls and waves a sheaf of papers in his hand. "Hear you this!" he cries. "I have in my hand a list of at least twelve subversives who are threatening an invasion of this great countryside of ours." A woman in long robes standing nearby tells us the stentorian words are those of Senator Mac Larckey. They ring out over the Edgartown rooftops from loudspeakers placed every few yards around the park's perimeter. Hermione's face draws into a tight scowl and straight trim to her lips. "Oh, this is no more than I have been expecting for a long time," she exclaims. "In my last magic potions class I learned that certain questionable persons on the Vineyard are exporting vast amounts of dried herbs and weeds which have been used for unthinkable purpose."

As the senator's voice hammers on, we hurry our pace for we have been told by several men and women along the way that the sanctuary toward which we hurry has been subject to an invasion by sundry weeds, vines, shrubs and growths of all kind not native to Martha's Vineyard. I pooh pooh the idea at first, thinking the Vineyard will always remain pure but Mac Larckey's speech is having a chilling effect on my normally optimistic enthusiasm. "Hermione's usually right when she develops an expectation," Harry cries. By now we are almost running from the park toward Pease's Point Way. Crowds have gathered and we hear voices speculating about calling out the Sheriff's Meadow Trustees, perhaps the Massachusetts Department of Environmental Affairs, even the National Guard. I wonder if my "pooh, pooh," has been a mite hasty.

"Now, go easy," I say. "We've heard scare tactics like this before. Remember the 1950's." Of course neither of my young companions has any recollection of that far back in our national history. They seem frightened but not surprised by the senator's words. Now I hear him saying, "In fact, I've just been advised that there are not just twelve subversives known to be hiding in Sheriff's Meadow; there may be as many as 60,000. At this I can see the crowd on Main Street has become excited. Several people are running to find a phone and a state policeman has come up the street from the court house unsnapping his holster, looking quite alarmed.

"Let's approach quietly and keep our wits about us," I caution. We have come to the small sign on Planting Field Way directing us to the right into the sanctuary. There is no place to park but a worn place on the grassy verge opposite the dirt path suggests some trespassers have been about in recent weeks. The tension in the air is thick and my heart pounds despite the calm demeanor I manage in order to comfort my young companions. Harry takes the lead and Hermione follows me. I am tempted to take her hand but she seems so self-possessed I decide the better part of valor is to give her the benefit of my trust that she can handle this adventure.

Hermione is a fount of knowledge. "Look;" (her eyes wide with vindication), look, there is Japanese knotweed over that fence. Look how it rises up, almost as if it is trying to get into the yard beyond. Oh my, this may be an omen of things to come."

I see handsome plumes at least eight feet in the air over the fence. The green stems and leaves are attractive like the shaggy tops wafting on the light air. We haven't gone another ten steps before Hermione points, not saying a word. We watch her deft fingers single out, among a variety of greens bordering the path, chinaberry, sometimes called porcelain berry. "This is getting to be serious," she says in a hush. Around a bend, her mood lightens when she points out another specimen. "There, honeysuckle, but that's quite benign. Besides I like the look of the blossoms, especially their smell." Our spirits are lifted a bit and we slog on.

By the time we come to the apex of our circular trail, Hermione is describing bitter sweet, "See, it's taking over everything in its path. Those oaks will be dead in a few seasons if that keeps up." Then, poke berry. Harry is brave enough to taste one but grimaces with the bitter taste and spits it out. "I'm afraid that may be poisonous," I warn. Harry seems none the worse for the taste. Now English ivy covers a huge patch of path-side ground. "Why, I always think this green triangular-leafed ivy is a great adornment to our yards and woods paths," I say. My optimism and enthusiasm seem to fall on deaf ears. "No, it's definitely not native." Hermione and Harry utter the words together, probably something they've learned at Hogwarts.

I can no longer hear anything coming from Main Street although a few voices seem to penetrate from around the edges of the sanctuary as if people are conversing on their porches unaware of us intruders in this quiet place. It is directly adjacent, after all, to the center of Edgartown in this flourishing summer season. Soon we see barberry with its red berries and fine thorns. I am not unhappy to learn this is another invasive. I have had too many experiences digging out prickers from my hands after trying to pull these varmints away from my outside shower stall.

I now turn my focus for a moment to other things besides invasive plants. We are standing on a tiny bridge over the stream which flows east into a small boggy looking pond. Our trail guide indicates it has a name, John Butler's Mud Hole. We have actually been following the trail around the inner Old Ice Pond. Beyond Butler's Mud Hole a stream, unseen from this distance, flows out to join Eel Pond, a small shallow bay protected by a narrow arm of sand on Nantucket Sound from the eastern end of Edgartown Harbor. We can see the State Beach and Oak Bluffs in the distance only as a faint blur.

"Look at the cat tails," I cry, finally identifying something ahead of my companions. "In Menemsha, we had these years ago but some wild grass with great plumes has taken over completely. I don't think I could find a single cat tail there now if I spent all day looking."

"There's your wild grass out there," calls an exultant Hermione, "Phragmites, the big plumes over to the left toward the salt water. The cat tails prefer fresh water and the phrag-mites the salt but they coexist close together for a time. The ones you see out there are on the march. Soon enough they will take over these cats close to the pond."

We haven't seen the senator's 60,000 invasives by any means but more than I had thought we would at first. "There's a happier side to this subject," Hermione says as we leave this lovely view and head back on the other side of the circle. "I can show you several wonderful natives who may yet survive if we can mount a sufficient counter attack on the invasives."

On the way back we are treated to a show of bone set, white clusters of buds with brush-like tufted flowers; jewel weed - mimicking tiny yellow orchids on long stems with nearly invis-ible brown spots within the blossom itself. Newcomb's "Wildflower Guide," which Harry carries in his pocket for such times, describes the fruit of these delicate blossoms as plump pods which explode their seeds when mature. Before we are fin-ished on the trail we see bay berry, smooth deep green leaves with berries not yet formed which will be an attractive gray.

"Wait, I say" certain that what I ask will be a puzzlement to everyone. "What about poison ivy? Isn't that the mother of all invasives?" Both Hermione and Harry are stunned. They stop and stare out into space as if summoning all the powers of wiz-ardry and magic they possess to be able to give me the proper answer. What about poison ivy, indeed.

Together they chime as one." There's no explaining P.I. It just is - that's all - it just is."

We return down the town streets enjoying views of meticu-lously kept gardens with early fall blooms. The town is quieter than when we first passed. The usual complement of summer tourists and locals going to work stride along the court house sidewalk. No stentorian tones ring out from loudspeakers. In fact, there are no loudspeakers. I ask, "What do you suppose has happened to all the people listening to Senator Mac Larckey wave his list of twelve, then 60,000, subversives about to invade the countryside. Neither Hermione nor Harry seems to hear me at first. I repeat myself. "What happened to Senator Mac Larckey?"

"Who in the world is Senator Mac Larckey?" they both scream together. "Are you O.K. or has the summer heat shriveled your brain?"

A puff of smoke envelops my head and I am afraid for an instant I will fall off balance. When the air clears I am standing alone. The scene around me has not otherwise changed. I walk puzzled to my car and drive home, lonely now, wondering about witchcraft and wizardry. Out by my garden wall in Menemsha, I spy yellow blooms on tall stems. I take a branch of jewel weed inside to show my wife. As I place it in a glass of water I touch one of the pods and it explodes with a tiny pop. I retrieve a round green seed from two feet away under the table.

[I am indebted to J.K. Rowling for the adventures of Harry Potter and his friends at Hogwarts School. I hope her second book "The Chamber of Secrets" waiting on my bedside table will not impair my judgment further or my ability to tell a straight story.]

HOW TO GET THERE: In Edgartown park your car on the street where allowed or at a town lot, walk or take the bus to Pease's Point Way on the Main Street side of Cannon Ball Park in Edgartown. Bike racks are available at the trail. No dogs. Proceed a short distance down Pease's Point Way until it becomes Planting Field Way, go another 0.2 mile and turn onto path at the sign on the right. An informative guide is available with map at the trail head.

Polly Hill Arboretum   Susan Safford

Polly Hill Arboretum

Polly Hill's front door has been left ajar in the "barn" at the arboretum bearing her name and I am ten minutes early. As I let myself in she swings out of the chair lift at the bottom of her stairs from the second floor to greet me. "It takes exactly 21 seconds to descend the stairs this way," she says, grasping my hand and making me feel entirely welcome. I am in for a treat this sunny day in the last week of September. Her niece, Heather Hillman, and newly appointed Director of Development, Tim Lasker, join us on a personalized tour. Mrs. Hill drives her small electric car with me in the front seat beside her; our two companions follow on foot.

"What sort of questions would you like me to answer?" she asks, turning the wheel into a faint track in the manicured grass path beyond the restored farm house now serving as offices, library and conference room.

"I'm not as interested in the details of the Polly Hill Arboretum as much as I am in your reactions and feelings as you make your rounds here. What is it like to have begun and maintained this place for so long?"

"I rejoice!" she says without a pause, stopping the car to look around. "I've worked to keep the plants comfortable and let them do what they want to do." In so saying she proceeds to direct a 90 minute non-stop tour of her own Garden of Eden. From the start I can see this is more than a collection of plants and trees which she has grown herself from seed or tiny seedlings and nurtured over the past forty or fifty years. This is one woman's lifetime and the breath of it still lives with gusto. Her voice is liquid and articulate as she rattles off the Latin names without a stumble or indecision for nearly every plant, shrub or tree we pass. "See this incense cedar I started in 1962." I crane my neck to look up at an immense tree with double trunks each at least a foot in diameter. "It grew where an old chicken house had stood for 300 years. Imagine the rich soil. Anything planted here has outgrown every thing planted elsewhere." She points to magnolias which are larger and fuller than their brothers and sisters just across the way.

"I love weeping things," she tells me. I think it's an odd comment for a woman who seems so outgoing and satisfied with her life. She points to her "valley of tears" with varieties of spruce, hemlock and beech which literally appear to be weeping. Their branches all dip over in a graceful arc toward the ground, I suppose evoking human form in melancholy attitude. I have to agree they are particularly handsome and unusual. We'll see several more of these varieties as we continue on our tour.

Just after we pass a rare fern leaf beech growing 30 feet in the air, obtained originally from tiny grafts which she bought "three for a dollar", we pause by a bare spot. With more excitement in her voice than usual, she points out some frail pink blooms in an otherwise bare patch (except for leaf mulch). "These are fall blooming cyclamen. Their leaves disappear during the winter and the area shows no growth in the spring. All season long we warn everyone not to step here. Now we're rewarded with the blooms." Two or three more such spots along the way harbor the same pink or white flowers. The path is now lined with huge camellias, their bright green leathery leaves as perfect as the illustrations in any catalogue. The shrubs are fat with red seed pods. "In the beginning I tried so hard to grow camellias and killed 40 of them," she says. My friends and acquaintances sent me samples from all over. Finally, through friends in the Camellia Society in Japan, I swapped some seeds and eventually got lucky." Luck does not seem quite the right word, I think. She points with particular pride to several Stewartias, a special genus related to camellias.

Suddenly we are shaded by tall Japanese hornbeam trees and come to what Mrs. Hill describes as her long dreamed of "allee" (the French word for passage or walkway, pronounced ah-LAY). Indeed it is a broad promenade guarded by tall trees, ending at another path which runs at right angles. There, at the far end, is a grouping of three boulders gleaned from a huge pile left on the property probably from original ground clearing. She has arranged them in the Japanese fashion for design and focus, the whole arrangement providing symmetry to this area of the garden.

Even Mrs. Hill must account for Vineyard marauders and the blueberry cage demonstrates her ingenuity at trying to save the berry crops from birds and deer. Thoroughly fenced and netted off on top, the patch of healthy bushes for reasons unknown has not produced well this year. At least we have one gardening experience in common, I think to myself. As if to turn attention away from this one seeming deficiency she steers to the base of a tree which has been measured recently at 61 and a half feet high, the tallest in the arboretum. "It's a metasequoia," she says," grown from a cutting 38 years ago." I try to imagine the changes she has seen in the time she has been nurturing this unique preserve. I was 35 years old when she planted this tree and what a wondrous supply of growth hormone it must have had. It is over six times as tall as I am at this moment and destined to attain perhaps 40 feet more.

By now I am beginning to think I should have brought a tape recorder. Information pours out of Polly, never pedantic, always tinged with a certain affection for the tree or plant she's describing, often with a personal note of the circumstances of its birth. The names she has given some of the plantings betray a true romantic at heart. "The tunnel of love," fashioned from espaliered Japanese hornbeams must have sheltered dozens of lovers passing under its bower. Farther along, red fruited dogwood seem to be everywhere overhead and a magnolia macro-phylla nearby with huge elephant-eared leaves bears pink avo-cado-sized fruit which soon will shed orange seeds.

"One of the gardeners asked me one day what the very green tree is called near the southern boundary wall. "See, over there," she says pointing. "That Nordman fir is the greenest tree in the place."

I'm impressed with the full stately tree loaded with its upright cones and top branches standing at least thirty feet high, unarguably the greenest tree around.. "Did you start it with only a seed?" I ask with some astonishment. Polly stops the car and reaches around for one of the white notebooks cataloguing every planting in the arboretum. Thumbing through the pages she tells me in less than a minute it was from a seedling. It's the only time she refers to her reference the whole morning.

Two chestnut trees come into view, one loaded with fruit encased in soft prickly light green jackets. These trees were planted by Polly's mother and sister. Polly first came to the Vineyard at age 16. In 1957 her mother died and Polly took over the care and management of this property. Her busiest develop-ment years were in the 1960's and 70's. Now, open spaces appear with well kept stone walls. "That's the Vineyard to me," Polly says, arresting the car's progress to make a point. "Open fields and stone walls - but I thought planting those tiny trees six feet apart would ensure space forever. I'll show how wrong you can be." We enter "Polly's Playpen" through a narrow latched gate, the name given this special deer-proof enclosure by her late hus-band, Julian. "The deer loved my azaleas, magnolias, camellias, everything else. One of my friends told me the only solution was to build a fence but it had to be ten feet tall. So Dan'l Manter and Arnie Fischer put it up in just two days. Later we had to add fine screen at the ground for baby rabbits. It's awful to have a baby rabbit inside the garden." Ahead lies a green path which originally had been six feet wide. Already we can see how the plant growth has encroached everywhere. The low naturally sculptured azaleas, the rhododendrons and magnolias alike have been free to "do what they will do" and have narrowed the path.

An unusual rhododendron attracts Polly's attention. She stops and caresses the leaves, turning them over to inspect the underside. "This is a hardy variety, called yak, from a high mountain on an island south of Japan." I can see its leaves are lighter than most. Still handling the leaves she says, "Rhododendron people are always turning leaves over to feel the underside."

"We use no sprays, do a lot of weeding, provide mulch and water - just keep everything as healthy as we can and let the plants take care of themselves."

I notice that, even on this fall day when nature is reclaiming much of its summer bounty, there is little evidence of unhealthy growth. Leaving by the second latched gate, Polly announces, "Now I'll show you where we store all our wealth." On the far side of a row of shrubs is a somewhat littered area containing leaf mulch, wood chips and piles of manure. Wealth indeed.

By this time, Heather has disappeared from our entourage. I assume she has things to do at home. Tim gamely walks along. Despite being on board at the arboretum only a short time he seems to have a lot of knowledge and asks good questions. Mrs. Hill shows no sign of tiring. "I'm the 'pet live fossil' around here," she says. "They treat me so well. Since the arboretum officially opened, I'm out of it all now but they call on me. I can help ... during winter we fax things back and forth. It's important to feel useful." Both Tim and I object to her remark about being out of it all. Polly Hill is in it all the way.

We come to a small enclosure with several dwarf varieties of trees. I ask if they are mistakes of nature. "If that's what you want to call them," she replies. "They're genetic variants." I think she doesn't like my word choice of mistakes. "You know," she continues, "I have had wonderful helpers here all my life. Some of the folks worked at various jobs for fifteen or twenty years."

We head back around the new Visitors Center toward the headquarters building. There are still things to see, the open spaces where trees have been removed or recently planted ones to enhance the new building on our left and Polly, showing her only exasperation this morning, points out the poison ivy and sassafras which are climbing either over or under the stone wall from the neighboring lot to encroach upon the arboretum. She turns to the other side of the path. "I love the conifers," she says. Look how they form a small grove. Weeds can't grow there. It's shaded and beautiful."

I decide that Julian's naming of Polly's playpen is apt. This arboretum has been a lifetime of work but it has taken on the character of entertainment, of passionate devotion, caring and nurturing, now a responsible handing over to others who will carry on all those features of her work. Not that Julian's word, play, implies less effort but it seems a better term for what Polly Hill does. She remembers everyone of her family and the origin of each, whether from seed, seedling or graft. Over the years she has left them in the fall on their own hoping to find them flourishing in the spring after a blustery Vineyard winter. That many did survive is testament, not only to her prowess as a devoted scientist but to her love and nurturing of each living thing.

As a final story she tells us about recently buying a fully developed shrub she fancied from a local nurseryman. When her friends saw it they said, "Imagine, Polly actually bought a tree, a whole tree!"

HOW TO GET THERE: The Polly Hill Arboretum is located on State Road in West Tisbury half-way between Humphrey's Bakery/Deli and the new Agricultural Hall. In season the Visitors Center is open 9:30 AM to 4:00 PM daily with regular daily tours. The grounds are open daily from sunrise to sun set except Wednesdays year-round. Fall tours will be conducted at 2 P.M. Saturdays and Sundays through the Columbus Day week-end, then will resume in the spring. Charge is $5.00 per adult. Members and children under twelve are free.

Peaked Hill Reservation
Tyson Trish

Radar Hill

These days after the eleventh of September are heavy, distracting us as we try against odds to reach back in time when routines were taken for granted. Quite unintentionally my walk this week propels me away from routine in a surprising way.

My walking companions to Peaked Hill Reservation, 73 acres of Martha's Vineyard Land Bank and Town of Chilmark property, are Diane and Tadao Arimoto of Pittsburgh. Early in our acquaintance with Diane (Wright) and her twin sister, Carol, they burst into our house in Vineyard Haven at eight o'clock one early July morning after driving all the way by themselves at age 16 from Pennsylvania. Of course they immediately called their parents to let them know of their arrival. By the mid seventies, Diane had introduced us to her new husband, Tadao (pronounced Ta-DOW), whom she had met while living and studying in Japan for several years. Now they are regular summer residents at the Wright home next door in Chilmark and are always ready for a walk, conversation, a meal or all three.

Although rain is threatened we don't hesitate to take off early morning to the joint Martha's Vineyard Land Bank-Town of Chilmark preserve at Peaked Hill, highest natural elevation (311 feet) on the Vineyard. Driving in from Tabor House Road near the land-fill, we pass recently cleared fields and stone walls. At the land bank sign we turn in and find a place to park, starting out on the blue trail to the overlook. Tadao and Diane utter great aahs and oohs as they step up on the rock platform to look over Vineyard Sound and some of the Elizabeth Islands. The height of the land here provides a stage in the air for a view in the midst of forest. We now look down at tree tops below us as the blue water shines beyond. Even better along the trail, the view opens up to Menemsha Bight and Lobsterville, Gay Head light and parts to the south.

Back in the woods we examine in detail Stonecutter's Rock. We begin to piece this huge erratic boulder (dumped at the terminus of the last great glacier 10 thousand years ago) back together from some mason's Herculean efforts to cut it down to size. We imagine how each of the enormous slabs at different angles from the parent boulder and each other can be made to fit together. Tadao thinks the chisel marks along the cut edges of granite are made by power tools. So, this is not such an ancient piece of work. Farther along the trail we come to Wee Devil's Bed, another erratic on its back with a surface depression imprinted by the sleeping giant.

Climbing the ridge of moraine running east to west we soon reach the view of views, looking 180 degrees from Edgartown and Chappaquiddick on the southeast to Cutty Hunk on the northwest. The table of land at this peak, formerly a federal station in World Wars I and II, has now been returned as near to nature as possible. Gone are the old sand bag revetment around the summit, the barracks for men and sheds for storage. A new tower being installed will enhance the Coast Guard's surveillance of the south side of the island for marine safety. Still remaining are uneven patches of macadam and cement foundations with various irons protruding. "Were there cannon here?" Tadao asks, looking out over the Atlantic. I have a twinge of wondering how this man, so recently of Japan, views this once American outpost of defense. The moment goes unmarked except for my demurral about cannon. "Only radar for aircraft and binoculars for watch, I think," is my response. I start to say that the soldiers probably carried light arms but remain silent. We walk through an overgrown field and dried-up fire pond planned for a large residential development in the 1970's. Various species of wild flowers bloom along the trail, yellow, pink, lavender. Suddenly the walk is finished at the parking lot but I realize my mind's attention remains on Radar Hill.

This morning, like so much in recent weeks since 9-11, has somehow been skewed by the terrorist attack in New York. I wonder if today's walk is the source of new confusion and unease. On the strength of my long friendship with the Arimotos, I ask Tadao to my home the next day with the understanding we'll have a conversation about his reactions to our viewing the site of the Army Signal Corps station at Radar Hill and the recent events in Manhattan. I ask him particularly to speak through his Japanese experience.

"I've been in this country nearly half of my life," he says early in our visit. "I came when I was 27. That was 25 years ago." Still a citizen of Japan, he is a registered alien with green card status. "My father was very conservative, a licensed Shinto priest, and worked for the emperor as calligrapher. He recorded all the emperor's speeches. He wore one of those pointy tuxedos every day of the week and attained a black belt in swordsmanship. During the war he sent the family to the country while he remained in Tokyo to defend his house when the invasion came." Tadao reports this with a little smile as if, in retrospect, that image of his father is anachronistic, quixotic at least, waiting with sword at the ready for American invaders.

Born in 1949, 4 years after the war, he thinks the American occupation lasted until he was about ten years old. He remembers the Army maintained their own bus line for soldiers and that his mother always told her children, "Never accept candy or chewing gum from the Americans." She remained bitter through her lifetime after her brother's death in the war. Tadao also became bitter toward his mother when she rejected Diane who was to become his wife. "Actually," he says, "My father was the first to accept Diane into the family and taught her calligraphy. On his death bed he called my mother to his side and whispered in her ear, 'Diane is a good girl.'" That seemed to moderate his mother's attitude somewhat during the many years she lived after that. "As far as the war goes," Tadao continues, "I can only feel pain for my immediate family. I never knew my uncle who died."

I ask him what he felt while we stood looking out over the south shore from the old radar installation. After a long pause, he says, "Sadness, I felt sadness. As far as a connection with September 11," he says, "before I came to this country I don't know whether I felt empathy with soldiers lost in war or not. [After 25 years] I can feel both cultures. I'm very sad and angry how vulnerable we are now to such a simple plot [the Trade Center bombing]. It's much easier to fight a known target, easier than sending troops to some country to find a few individuals. I'm angry, uneasy."

I am impressed how he says "how vulnerable WE are." We sit quietly for a time and he continues, "If some guys in England came to U.S. and committed terrorist act, would U.S. send troops to England? Seems to be different reactions to different countries, different people."

Tadao tells how, at age 9 or 10, he formed a strong impression of Americans which has never changed. His oldest brother brought an American intelligence agent home for dinner one evening. The Arimoto home, in Japanese style, had rather low ceilings and, during dinner a mouse which lived in the walls ran across the ceiling just above the family assembled to entertain the American. The adults cringed with embarrassment, Tadao remembers, except the American, who, using his limited command of Japanese, looked up at the mouse and said the word "ghost" with a questioning rise of inflection for all to understand as a joke. He broke the tension much to the relief of everyone present. "A Japanese would never have made light of such an incident," Tadao says. "He would have joined in the embarrassed silence and the family would have felt humiliated."

"What prejudice have you run into in the United States?" I ask him. Again a long silence before he responds. "You know, don't you, that Pennsylvania has the largest number of Ku Klux Klan members in the country?" I am surprised but he has lived there for 25 years and may know this. Tadao is a skilled wood craftsman and makes modern furniture, cabinets, tables and chairs, often of exotic wood, in his own small company in Pittsburgh. Some of his work graces the library at the University of Pittsburgh and he is a prize winner at several artisans' shows in the area. "I buy my woods often in the remotest parts of the state," he goes on, "rural areas where the Klan is often common. I never run into any problem at all. But, in a group of Japanese when we are all speaking in Japanese, I have been asked to leave a restaurant or bar because we offend others present." Tadao seems to take this with little rancor. "I do not get into trouble when I am alone, only when I go along in a group."

He tells me about his experience teaching in a trade school in Pittsburgh. "I never have a problem myself even though the school is in the tough part of town. Students are all adults 18 to 54; some come from halfway houses after prison, some are addicts in recovery. I once stopped a fight between two whites carrying knives. I took their knives away and made them fight with fists at the end of the hallway. They didn't want to keep it up after that." Somewhere in this conversation, Tadao tells me he thinks the Asian face is less threatening than others. Perhaps he is lucky.

The confusion and unease I felt a day ago after Radar Hill has been diffused this morning. The discovery of a side of my friend, never explored before, came easily. The 11th of September may have given us more than the frightening sense of vulnerability as Tadao suggests. I think by putting aside the fear of exploring new ways of thinking and talking we may be propelled into a more thoughtful exploration of the human condition which places war and peace, black and white, foreign and native, along with many other facets of human interaction, in the same kettle of fish. Without exploring the otherness of Tadao Arimoto, I would not have discovered his sameness.

HOW TO GET THERE: Take the State Road (South Road) up-Island to Beetlebung Corner in Chilmark Center. Turn right and immediately take the sharp right onto Middle Road which starts you back down-Island for about a mile to Tabor House Road. Turn left, drive 0.5 miles to the entrance land bank logo for Peaked Hill on the left. Follow the dirt road 0.7 miles, bearing right at each intersection. Turn right at the Open Land Foundation sign and park in the small area reserved at the trail head. A map of the trails is posted on the bulletin board and hand-held maps under plastic are available to borrow while you walk.

Great Rock Bight

Ralph Stewart

Great Rock Bight with Tom Vogl

Question: what commences with a pale green chameleon, a tiny cordon bleu, gold fish and a variety of special chickens who at times roam free over the panhandle in West Tisbury? I arrive at the Long-Vogl residence an hour early for my walk with Tom Vogl, and, as if I were on time to the minute, Katherine Long invites me on a tour of her remarkable home. We inspect an aviary, a weaving area complete with loom, and a living room lined with shelves holding 800 cook books. A library ladder stands alongside to reach the topmost volumes. Their sun room is home to a shy pale green chameleon and small blue finch. The field out back holds horse-trough tanks for gold fish plus house and coops for the fowl - silver Dorkings which Julius Caesar brought from Rome and were named for the English town, mottled Houdans, gold penciled Hamburgs (called "hats"), crested Polish and, finally, Buttercups (hardly distinguishable from the "hats"). This is the start of my afternoon with Katherine's husband, Tom, who arrives as several of the chickens begin to flit past me at the gate into the great outdoors.

I've known Tom Vogl for 3 or 4 years, meeting Friday mornings at the hospital for Medical Rounds. He is a quiet sort, says little at these conferences but is a store of knowledge about computers which he has demonstrated to me when I've crashed one way or another. I hope to pick his brains about his life as a scientist. We choose Great Rock Bight, the Martha's Vineyard Land Bank Preserve off North Road in Chilmark, because he's never visited there. Early fog has blown away, skies are mostly clear, wind is up and temperature is 70 degrees. We launch the walk and conversation.

"Using the retrospectroscope," he says, "I guess I spent almost all my life being involved with photons." While an undergraduate at Columbia in New York, he studied physics, chemistry, geology and enough upper level courses to graduate. His student research with crystals involved the study of uranium ore, sklowdowskite, named after Marie Curie's maiden name. "At one point, I was invited back at a 'munificent' salary to work on my advanced degree. They only wanted me because I knew how to install sinks," he says with a characteristic laugh. Apparently he kept the x-ray department going by installing and servicing developing tanks for x-ray film. Having had enough of school, he went instead full time at Westinghouse in Pittsburgh where, in addition, he earned a Masters in Physics at University of Pittsburgh and a Ph.D. in Systems Science at Carnegie Mellon. His work there involved infra-red detection devices for military use in night vision. "It was never successful." he says, "but interesting and pretty good physics." For a time he worked in California at the Hughes Research Labs and from his window in Malibu he could watch whales spouting off shore. It was the time Theodore Maiman shot off his first laser. Tom soon returned to Pittsburgh and Westinghouse to resume work on infra-red detection and design of optical systems with one of the 20th century's great lens designers, David Gray. The computer programs worked out at that time are still used by Japanese manufacturers in designing lenses for their cameras.

Colleagues from General Electric, Bell Labs and he would jokingly agree when interviewing prospective employees that they would have everything a university can offer except the opportunity to grade papers. "Unfortunately that's no longer true anywhere," he adds. From lenses Tom switched to an interest in biological effects of light and its use in new-born infant jaundice. By now, Tom had become Adjunct Professor of Pediatrics and Radiology at Columbia College of Physicians and Surgeons, where he joined the study of babies with too much circulating yellow pigment, thus jaundice, due to insufficient metabolism in their immature liver system. The problem, if severe, causes brain damage and plagued medical scientists for years. "Actually [our work] came about through an interesting story [not related to this particular work]. My father, Alfred Vogl, as a resident physician in Vienna in the thirties was responsible for the syphilitic ward. Mercurials (mercury) were the primary treatment at the time. Nurses were extremely meticulous, even about their records. They noticed after the mercury injections, the patients' urine output went up like crazy."

"Dr. Vogl became the father of mercurial diuretics," I conclude, and Tom agrees. Ironically, a similar story developed around the observations by nurses in a London lying-in hospital who noticed that jaundiced infants in the nursery occupying cribs next to the windows were always less jaundiced than the ones in the back of the room. Subsequently doctors were able to demonstrate, first on rats, then on the babies themselves, that light rays hastened the decline in jaundice while awaiting the babies' own livers to mature and take care of the problem naturally. Many were spared the more invasive and potentially dangerous treatment of exchange transfusions.

I am curious how Tom, without a medical degree, was received by medical colleagues after assuming the position of a professor of medicine. "It went very well. I had a grand time. Nominally I was a full professor and had several graduate students in bio-engineering who were getting degrees under me. I was like a civilian employed in the military with equal rank. I got a lot of papers written, over a hundred-fifty I think."

"Oh, isn't this gorgeous!" Tom interrupts his steady stream of recollections. We have come suddenly out of the woods onto a small platform overlooking Vineyard Sound and the small curved beach and great rock beyond. During our walk we have been aware of the steady beat of the wind through the fall leaves. The ground is littered. We stop a moment to read the inscription on the brass tablet honoring the Chilmark slave, Rebecca, Woman of Africa, along the African-American Heritage Trail. I tell the story of how Rebecca's granddaughter becomes the mother of the first African-American whaling captain from Edgartown in the 19th century. Now we're ready to descend the steep stairs to the beach.

Although Tom left P&S before the light work was completed, he had had a hand in advancing that important tool in Medicine. A National Academy of Sciences offer was too attractive to turn down and he found himself in Washington helping to write a report of work on photo-therapy. Later he helped in the final report on toxicity of the anesthetic called Halothane which led to the replacement of that drug by better and safer agents. "I left after four years. Not many people stayed that long."

We are now on the beach with a long view to the east down-island. Haze obscures the Elizabeths to a degree but the views are spectacular. Tom stops to take a picture. We walk west along large irregular stones and run the risk of breaking a leg or worse. We retreat to the smooth sand and back up the stairs to the trail. Winded, we sit on a bench and catch our breaths. "Another funny story came out of my work on crystals at Westinghouse. This goes back a few decades," Tom begins. "It turns out that my name is on the original patent of the first temperature sensing device which has evolved into those strips of paper you stick on fish tanks to track temperature."

"And all the strips that mothers use to take babies' temperature?" I ask. "Oh, yes," he says. "I got a pat on the back, a framed certificate and a dollar." We both laughed over his large reward. He was soon asked to be executive secretary of a national Commission on Digestive Diseases at NIH, "the hardest work I ever did," he admits now. "Never home on weekends but it was a good report and the field got more money [for research] out of it. I was too exhausted to look for another job so I stayed on and helped run the interagency coordination on nutrition research which was largely run out of President Carter's White House. In eight years I figured I had about one year's experience. With new committee members from Congress elected each year I would have to start explaining from scratch [annually]. I wanted to get back to doing my own research. Basically I get bored every ten or fifteen years and need to change fields."

On the advice of a friend, Tom went to see Dan Alkon who was working in a small unit of the NIH at the Marine Biological Lab in Woods Hole. "After sitting on a bench outside MBL talking with Alkon for an afternoon about the biochemical and biophysical basis of learning, I decided, now that sounds like something I'd be interested in." His next 16 years were spent with both Office of Naval Research and NIH support doing computer modeling of associative memory and memory at the cellular and sub-cellular level having a grand time."

I am now well over my head in trying to understand where this research might go and tell Tom so. "There has to be a permanent change in the brain of some sort, and that turns out to be a change in a neurotransmitter channel commonly known by the initials GABA for gamma amino butyric acid. You cannot learn a fact. All you can have is an association of facts. The first facts are probably associations of feelings between intra-uterine fetuses with their mother, sounds or touch through the mother's abdominal wall and chemical changes within the uterus."

Another bench invites us to rest and talk of family and house hunting, our own stories of first arrival on the Vineyard. Tom's parents and brothers and sister escaped Nazi Germany in the mid 30's through Italy and England before finally coming to the

United States just before Dunkirk, a year before Pearl Harbor. The elder Vogl's journey is a story in itself, getting out of Europe "by the skin of his teeth," repeating medical school in Edinburgh, finally establishing himself in practice and for the rest of his life past 80 as Professor of Medicine at New York University and Mt. Sinai Hospital in New York.

As I leave my friend off in West Tisbury, I think of the shelves of cook books back at the house. All those books! Tom's story comes back to me. "One day Katherine found beet greens and squid in our refrigerator while planning dinner. We both remembered seeing a recipe including these items somewhere but it took us two or three hours to find it. We decided then to catalogue all our recipes by ingredients. PC's were just coming out and it took 4 months to find the software package we wanted. We now have 8000 recipes on our hard drive. You can view the most delicious ones on our web site."

Our last conversation touches on September 11 and the Trade Center Towers attack but it is time today simply to enjoy this brief respite from bad news and look forward to Winter Solstice, the anniversary 21 years ago of Tom's and Katherine's first meeting. I can't wait to get back into their house to explore more.

HOW TO GET THERE: Drive on State Road up-island just past Humphrey's Bakery and Deli in West Tisbury and turn right on North Road. Proceed 1.2 mile beyond Tea Lane and turn right at Land Bank logo, drive 0.5 mile to park. From Chilmark, drive down North Road 0.3 mile past Tabor House Road to the Land Bank sign on the left.

Beach at Menemsha Hills   Susan Safford

Walking Menemsha Hills

"The sun all but disappears save yellow spots flashing at tree top; then a fringe of light covers the canopy."

Exactly one mile down the North Road from the Menemsha Cross Road, on my left, a compact green and white sign announces the entrance up a steep drive to Menemsha Hills, maintained by The Trustees of Reservations.

Today's dawn quiet is hassled by northwest winds which have blown out from Cuttyhunk for a day and a half. I'm still sleepy but the incandescence from Nantucket in the southeast is just beginning to touch some of the tree tops on Prospect Hill. The parking lot is empty, and I brush past the bulletin case and start climbing.

The oaks overhead, clinging to their parchment leaves, are whistling and waving. My mind and sight are clearing by the minute. Three hundred and fifteen feet do not make a strenuous climb, but my breath comes faster and my chest feels the comfortable expansion of good air. When the surrounding blue water opens up suddenly on three sides of me, I'm struck for the thousandth time by the crystalline beauty of this Island in the sea. Oaks and low-lying shrubs hug the ground on the exposed hilltop as if pruned by the drying winds. Off to the southeast, where the sun now glows yellow-white, Nantucket Sound stretches into haze. Isolated rooftops lead my eye toward Nomans Land hidden behind the corner of Squibnocket, to Gay Head — the familiar line of utility poles at Lobsterville — Dog Fish Bar, Menemsha Bight, and the Elizabeths, now to the northeast. The long thin strand of the eastern projection of Cuttyhunk is visible from this height. It disappears from view at home near sea level. Nashawena abuts Cuttyhunk to the right and Pasque (I've always confused its order on the horizon until today) is third in line. This panorama alone is worth the early rising but I press on with my walk.

Down from the summit, oaks dominate. The sun all but disappears save yellow spots flashing at tree top; then a fringe of light covers the canopy. Its floor takes on the day. The trees here are tall and old, but when I emerge nearer the shore, their tops are sculpted like skullcaps by the winds from the west, arching with grace over the hillsides. Now the oaks mix with beetlebungs, pine and maple, blueberry and bayberry. A grove of beetlebungs is swept clean underneath. A phalanx of frost-burned ferns stands a last guard, around its bare soldier trunks. The ferns retain their grace and lacy detail despite a death sentence of impending winter.

I remember nine years ago — my last sojourn here — water over my sneakers in marshy low spots, now brown and dry. The board walks are only an added convenience today. Next May they'll keep me dry.

Wind is the only noise. I am out of range of cars on North Road and the rare fishing boat I glimpse in the sea. The birds have gone. Only a deer print now and then betrays the presence of other life here. Suddenly a sharp small crack over my shoulder alerts me. I see nothing different. Perhaps that deer is watching my progress and I'm not alone.

At a mile and a half I'm standing on a platform at the northeast corner of the reservation. Woods Hole and Falmouth are in the distance. The lonely chimney stub of the brickworks at Roaring Brook stands sentinel below. The growth surrounding it is higher than I remember. The chimney seems to be disappearing from the landscape — one more vanishing trace of a life long retired from the Vineyard. The thought of firing bricks fires my romance with olden times. I see smoke from that stack and piles of clay, men moving about stacking red bricks on pallets in back and a yoke of oxen hauling the day's production up from the beach. Along the way I'd seen great erratics dropped by the glacier. Other ox carts once traveled here carrying these boulders to the seaside for ripraps and jetties to protect the land.

Now the path steepens toward the shore. I see the sound — blue and choppy under the wind. Rain has taken its toll in the gullies, but the long-used tracks hold up pretty well. Lifting myself down the last 50 yards into the wash-outs now dry, I reach the stony beach and look back to the high bluff on my right. Nearly vertical, it seems a little less steep than last time. The topmost reaches are covered with clots of grass clinging to their sandy base against the ravages of wind and rain and tides.

The trek back around another loop of path finally intersects with my old footsteps. Retracing them brings me home. The sound of workmen's hammering and the singing tires on North Road suddenly intrude. I am returned after 90 minutes from another world, another time. I've reacquainted myself with geography, pristine dawn, waves and wind, Pasque and its order on the horizon, the oaks and beetlebungs, a watchful deer.

HOW TO GET THERE: Drive on North Road toward Chilmark and go 0.6 miles past Tabor House Road. On the right you will find the entrance to Menemsha Hills marked by the Trustees logo. Turn in and park in the area provided at the top of the hill.

The Tabernacle

Bob Schellhammer

Wesleyan Grove

Imagine stretching your mind a century and a half to the mid-1800's on a hot July afternoon under a two and a half ton canvas tent in the middle of Wesleyan Grove. You are at the northern expanse of wooded countryside in Edgartown near a sandy bluff which overlooks Nantucket Sound. A fiery Methodist preacher stands atop a roofed board platform and you are in the midst of 1500 other sweating souls seated on crude backless benches. You listen to brimstone words describing the road either to sin or salvation. The time is the height of the religious revival in America and a message of personal salvation is being visited on the "vice ridden whaling port" of Edgartown. (Until 1880, the town we now know as Oak Bluffs remained a part of Edgartown. From 1880 to 1908 it was Cottage City and thereafter, to the consternation of some old-timers still alive, Oak Bluffs.)

By mid-century the area around a huge canvas-covered tabernacle holds dozens of white peaked tents pitched on platforms with wooden side walls, board walks in front of them, arranged in concentric circles about the three acre plot sanctified for religious observance, called from the start Wesleyan Grove. Methodists largely foster the camp meeting movement from its invention in 1800. Baptists and Presbyterians who participate earlier largely drop away. By 1844, Methodists have increased their members to more than a million from no more than 2800 in the year 1800. Although the church itself doesn't recognizes camp meetings as part of official Methodism, nevertheless, they become an important activity, a source of newly converted members and eventually a well recognized respite, especially at the seashore. A camp meeting manual of the times pronounces that," ... human life needs to be dotted over with occasions of stirring interest, ... its watering places along the way ... ." Weekend attendance at Wesleyan Grove will reach to 3500, sometimes 5000.

Several weeks in a tent are an adventure without question. Despite Victorian attitudes about modesty, families somehow remain on speaking terms with each other and return summer after summer for revival. The Methodist message is strong indeed. Much time is spent on the hard seats under the eye of the preacher. Success of a given camp meeting is measured by the number of those coming forward for personal salvation and the number of backsliders who return to grace in Methodism. These are not entirely dry and endless sermons. The preacher's ability to exhort may be potent and the emotion provoked is often loud and the weeping riveting, sometimes with swooning and hysteria. At other times, members tire of the sermon and hard seats, retire to smaller groups in the tents holding more intimate meetings by themselves. As the evening progresses, the shouts of those finally convinced of their need for conversion are heard across the expansive camp.

As the years pass, I can imagine the tents beginning to be replaced by small wooden box houses about the same size and shape and on the same lots as their canvas predecessors. I pass the first such cottage, pre-fabricated in Connecticut and erected in 1876. I see workmen moving two of these tiny buildings joining them front to back. The framing is simple, a stout four-by-four inside each corner and wide vertical pine boards walling in the sides. Spaces for doors and windows are simply cut out to size, the sash or door frame inserted without headers above. With minimal work there is not only a living room open to the central tabernacle in front through wide double doors, but a bedroom in the back. Cooking is still done outside. Privies remain in the lot behind the house. Eventually as the tents are replaced altogether, other simple sheds are grafted on to the back or to the side providing finally a kitchen and, then, second stories sprout with two or three tandem bedrooms above. A narrow stair, steep as a cliff, is built on the side, sometimes descending on an outside wall requiring the would-be sleeper to leave the house and enter the staircase through another door.

Still in an imaginative mood, stretch further your mind and walk through the camp grounds today coming in off Circuit Avenue through the narrow arch of Tabernacle Avenue into Trinity Park, the modern name given to the original Wesleyan Grove. I go on a light-filtered day after the full moon of the night before, my head full of conversation with a long-time resident of the camp grounds and pictures of maps and anecdotes from my favorite correspondent in Oak Bluffs. Summer has finished and the leaves from the tall oak trees have spread a thick blanket across the lawn. The canvas-covered meeting area has been replaced by the great Iron Tabernacle, barged to the island and erected in the grove, in 1879, its immense illuminated cross pointing to the sky ever since. Today, despite the occasional groan of an immense earth moving machine or the clang of metal, either from Oak Bluffs workmen digging their new sewer system or the nearby renovations to the open-sided tabernacle, a sense of vacancy, of repose and quiet overlies the deserted paths and streets.

The present here is a step back in time. The many vacant homes in this season of impending winter encourage a ghostly look. Of 312 cottages (down from 500 in 1880), about 35 are occupied during the winter. Their dazzle remains but being empty allows the viewer a more relaxed and closer look. Sharp peaked roofs, their narrowness, front porches overhung by galleries, the slim space between neighbors and the arrangement in rather hit or miss circular lanes, crisscrossing and turning at odd angles, intrigue the walker. I retrace my steps three different times thinking I am taking a new path. The name

Commonwealth Avenue conjures the broad two-aisled boulevard in Boston with a handsome greensward between. Here at the camp grounds it is no more than a double foot path with barriers at each end to allow only bikers and pedestrians to pass. I remember making a house call to Clinton Avenue many years ago on a dark night, totally lost. I wonder now how I ever found the house, especially since I had to walk to find the patient's front door. Washington Park has been renamed Victorian Park. Several streets bear new names in the interest of correcting duplication in Oak Bluffs and so that police and fire trucks may find their way. These up-to-date changes have broken the hearts of some long-time residents. Miraculously, I think as I see the closeness of these small structures, only two houses have burned in the whole area.

I begin to note the colors on the gaily painted cottages. Most have at least three shades, some four, a few five: purple, bright or dull; blue, robin's egg and royal; white of course but never alone; pink and pink and pink; yellows, tans and ochre; cerise, gray, reds of any kind, even aqua. The invention of the jigsaw early in the 19th century fostered the development of American Carpenter Gothic architecture exemplified in all these camp ground cottages I pass. The device consisted of a huge wheel connected by belt to a tiny wheel which in turn oscillated a saw blade, powered by vigorous foot pedaling. Evidence of the ingenuity of local artisans is plentiful here: hearts in abundance: sunbursts; flowers - daisies, zinnias, mythic pendants or animals, and geometrics of all variety.

This colorful place which Jeremiah Pease of Edgartown founded one hundred-sixty-five years ago remains still an active summer colony around the great tabernacle, even with a scattering of year-round residents. Its name is now generally called by islanders Oak Bluffs Camp Grounds although the official name remains Martha's Vineyard Camp Meeting Association (MVCMA).

Few people today I think know that Wesleyan Grove was the first of three summer areas to be developed in 1835. Soon after that, four Vineyard whaling captains and two off-islanders bought 75 acres of land just to the south of Wesleyan Grove while the more conservative camp meeting members hesitated doing the same to protect their position on the grounds that "it would be too worldly". Their mistake seemed obvious when the new folks soon offered up 1000 house lots for sale. How our present-day M.V. Commission would have gasped at this maneuver! Hence the "city" of Oak Bluffs, adjacent to the camp grounds, was born. The new Circuit Avenue truly circuited the new town from its present location easterly to the ocean bluffs, then following the beach south to what is now South Circuit Avenue and back west and north again to the area beyond the current Oak Bluffs Library. Oak Bluffs was sin-city to the Methodists of the camp grounds. They built an eight foot fence on the border with Oak Bluffs to isolate themselves. Gates were locked at ten o-clock and any evening revelers risked life and limb to climb through a loose fence slat or confront an angry mother waiting at their cottage door.

The third development was the Vineyard Highlands on the bluff near the present East Chop Beach Club. There, eventually, the Baptists erected their own wooden tabernacle and surrounding camp ground. By 1880 these three settlements, irked at poor services supplied by the town of Edgartown and the taxes levied therefor, successfully seceded and formed Cottage City. The name was changed back again to Oak Bluffs in 1908.

In 1879, the great iron tabernacle originally cost $7,147.84. It now requires an estimated $2 million for refurbishing, of which $1.56 million has been pledged already. New tin shingles adorn the entrance arcade and housing for a modern public address system. I circle the big open-air pavilion to the tune of hammers and shouts from the carpenters on the roof made of corrugated asbestos and still sound, re-anchored with 10,000 new screws. Old benches from the original tent tabernacle grace the back of the sitting area. At least they have backs to them now I think. You must arrive early for events here in order to get the more comfortable seats up front. The Methodists must have thought to keep the worshippers a little on edge, awake and invested in the goings-on at the podium. The big cross atop the cupola has rested there since 1984, having replaced one destroyed in the winter of 1967-8. That one was 11 feet 5 inches high and 7 feet 3 inches wide weighing 350 pounds and illuminated by 66 light bulbs. The original solid cross was erected in 1926, all the previous ones represented in red on a flying banner at the tip of the tower.

I am on a tour with Albion Hart, a fourth generation Vineyarder now residing year-round on Trinity Park and functioning as de facto camp meeting historian.

The Trinity Methodist Church, across from Trinity Park and built a year before the tabernacle, likewise is undergoing a substantial face-lift, estimated to cost $250,000, $175,000 already pledged. We inspect the south wall where outside asbestos sheathing has been removed for a look at the underlying clapboards to see if they are worth saving. The process for disposal of the asbestos is involved and expensive, wrapped in heavy plastic before shipping out to a processor who grinds up the material and buries it deep in the ground from whence it came. Inside, Mr. Hart points to the stained glass already repaired and the empty spaces for sash still in the Chilmark work shop of Heidi Dunkl. A photo depicts her at the painstaking work on her bench. The pew backs, dark oak probably, are each fashioned with one extraordinarily wide plank. The lofty ceiling and wall finishes are of tin. Victorian lamps hang on long chains from above. This "chapel" was the winter church, the tabernacle the summer church in years gone by.

The ancient organizations here about Trinity Park are going strong into the 21st century. Not so apparent from these external features are the changes the camp meeting itself has undergone. In the beginning, the 21 members of the board of directors were all Methodist ministers; now there are but two clergy. The year 1931 saw the change of the MVCMA from a legally religious institution to an interdenominational one, where only the board need still be Protestant. "It's much more ecumenical these days," Mr. Hart tells me. "But there is still a spirit here unchanged. You can feel it. I used to talk to all the leaseholders as they acquired cottages here." (The land on which they sit is leased from MVCMA.) "I'd tell them I hoped they would catch that spirit and keep it. I think most of us have." At the camp grounds centennial in 1979 Reverend George H. Moseley called on camp meeting members to "renew our covenant and consecrate this Tabernacle anew ... to receive and welcome all ... without regard to race, nationality, denomination or any other divisive distinction of this world."

Fourth or fifth, even sixth generation of camp grounders keep coming by force of their roots, this place one of the few places on earth that has changed so little over time. Fortunately the privies have been replaced by septic systems, now about to be further upgraded by the new sewer; running water from the town instead of five or six wooden and iron pumps scattered throughout the small parks; electricity instead of whale oil and kerosene. Cottages have been enlarged to house indoor toilets and kitchens and two or more buildings have been combined to give more comfortable space. Even so, the closeness of everyone dilutes the privacy that many people would feel unacceptable. Still the spirit of the camp grounds seems to overcome those disadvantages.

Word has it that occasionally a household gone to bed at Trinity Park will look up at the windows facing the park to see tourists peering into the dark cottage thinking no one is in residence. They simply pull the bed covers up over their heads and stay quiet until the trespassers pass on. "I like the tourists," one cottager tells me after living here over twenty years. "I've been a tourist all over the world looking at folks sitting on their porches, working in their gardens, walking on their sidewalk. I love to meet them, answer their questions. Some people think we're paid to stay here, sit on our porches to entertain the tourists."

I can't help thinking these cottagers have it right. They've saved a wonderful space and above all they've remained a community, no longer all of the same religious persuasion, no fiery Methodist preacher bellowing forth on Sundays in the old nineteenth century revival fashion but I would bet most of them have caught the spirit of the camp grounds. Their generations of roots help keep it alive for themselves, even the newcomers.

My step into the century-before-last has been as real as if I had been there, minus perhaps the smells and women's bustles. Where else in our busy world could I find a place more serene than this? I leave Wesleyan Grove with the strains of the old hymn, "Faith of Our Fathers," peeled out from the belfry of Trinity Methodist Church, fading gradually from my ears but embedded in that echoing area of my brain that once in a while sings a tune during every waking moment when all is otherwise quiet.

[I am indebted to Robert Hughes of Oak Bluffs for many mailings of historic and anecdotal interest about Oak Bluffs and the island; to Albion Hart of "Hartsease," Trinity Circle, for his generosity of time and information, particularly for pointing me to Ellen Weiss's book, "City in the Woods," from which I have gathered much information about the origins and early activities and conditions existing in the early days of Wesleyan Grove for use in this article.]

HOW TO GET THERE: Walk up the main street in Oak Bluffs, Circuit Avenue, on the right side until you reach The Secret Garden, a store on the corner of Tabernacle Avenue. Turn right and follow sign through the entrance to Martha's Vineyard Camp Meeting Grounds. Trinity Park is the site of the great outdoor tabernacle.

WINTER

Snow flakes hurl themselves against the window and slide down the pane. After a few minutes snow gives way to a constant drizzle, enough to cancel my walk this typically winter morning. Perhaps there is no typical day. Another will be crisp and clear with bright sun and not a breath stirring. I'll walk at Menemsha Hills on that sort of day and look up through motionless tree limbs to the blue sky and hear every step the wild creatures take on the forest floor.

A January walk out to Long Point in West Tisbury becomes an adventure when the wind's up. You hear its steady moan and the surf's pounding. The sensations abound in your head and ears, nothing like you experience away from the shore. Sand blows stingingly through cuts in the dunes and white foam piles up on the beach. You trudge bent forward to keep upright and your shoes dig deeply into the sand. On a quiet day, you feel the warmth of the sun as you walk along Gay Head beach in late afternoon and watch the orange sun slip below the ocean. In those early moments after sunset, gorgeous colors change by the minute, rosy red to orange to mauve and then gray. Then the cold returns and you walk back to the car confirmed that winter remains.

Birds are less varied in winter but our feeder remains active, often frenzied before a storm, when all of the neighborhood are alive with the activity of feeding in time to return to a shelter. Gold finches are less gold but still scrappy. White throated sparrows, wandering juncos, and always the chickadees abound. Snow cover sets off the cardinals almost too brightly to be true. I stand with aching arm outstretched for several minutes to be rewarded occasionally by a friendly chickadee lighting on my hand to take a sunflower seed or two. My inner almanac forecasts the first week of January as the coldest of the year. Outside faucets, forgotten in the fall clean-up and closings, are apt to burst after rare sub-zero temperatures. But a night when you venture out past the back porch with lights off suspends you in a world of your own. Never are the stars so bright or is the full moon more glorious as in a cloudless winter sky. I hurry back to the fire after a few minutes of watching. The reward by the hearth is plenty for taking such chilly moments. The February (or January) thaw won't last long and, until the ground hog lets us know, we have no idea really when this season will end.

"What do you do all winter?" a visiting friend asks. "Well, I don't know ..." I answer and then dribble off into a long recitation. By the time one goes to church if that's his persuasion, and works a five day week or even a three day week or even a retired sort of non-work week, tinkering several hours a day, there is too much to do: political jobs like the board of health or selectman's office, volunteer jobs like meals-on-wheels, or the hospital gift shop, island chorus or church choir, fishing and fishing and fishing, hunting in winter and quahogging in October, ice skating, the Rotary Club, the Lions, the Red Men, Zonta Club, libraries, crafts, painting, writing, walking, jogging, to say nothing of endless town meetings and committees. I've been retired from Medicine for several years and I find astonishing my inability to fathom ever having worked a steady week.

Winter is the time when the roads are empty of cars except at the coming and going times for work. I ride the length of North Road after 9 pm and meet only a car or two. It is the time when regular and part-time residents disappear to Naples, Florida, or Naples, Italy, Arizona, California, New York City, or an apartment in Boston. A hardy band of commuters to the mainland are prominent, mornings playing poker at the foot of the forward port stairway on the Islander, or nursing a cup of coffee to wake up enough to drive onto the Cape or Providence. By evening they are socializing with fellow commuters and many others they usually know at least by sight if not by name. It's a change from summer when we recognize hardly anyone on board at all.

By late February the days finally are noticeably longer, snow melts quickly, although we may have a blizzard in March, but the north-bound great blue heron in our marsh of winter becomes a frequent passer-through, a sure sign the weather will soon warm.

Me and Waskosim's Rock   Ralph Stewart

Waskosim's Rock

I drive down the North Road six days out of seven. It's a rare day which doesn't find a car or two in the small lot on the south side of the road, the trail head for Waskosim's Rock Reservation. The off-season is no exception for this Martha's Vineyard Land Bank's 185 acre preserve.

The trails provide several comfortable walks. Today is in the forties and gray overcast. I scan the bulletin board and see messages which bring a smile: "too many cig butts," [which I never noticed] " huge showy holly," [I wonder which one the writer means] "Merry Xmas and Happy New Year," [of course!,] "Watch for the cougar," [Now, that brings a little rush.] "skunk cabbage up, Jan 1," [Darn, someone beat me to it this year and, finally] "George were here ... ," [Some good soul had obviously tried to erase all these old messages and the writing was unclear; could he have meant, "Wish George [Mills] were here?" ... a fellow poet.] I pocket the handy plastic-sealed map. Lilly and I hurry along. Dogs are leashed at the trail head. Later, a friendly sign says O.K., just keep your dog within voice control or in sight while you're here.

The woods on a thawing January morning are quiet, none of the rustling leaves and cracking twigs of the late fall, strangely, neither any aroma of decomposing vegetation that filled the air two months ago. My footfalls are hushed. Lilly and I don't speak. She's in Heaven. The woods are stark and my sight line is increased by fathoms. The stone walls running through woods and up hills remind me of the labors of generations of men and boys past who cleared these woods the first time to make way for their grazing sheep and cattle. If these folks came back today, would they groan at the sight of their lost labors, the woods reclaiming hard fought-for fields? I round a turn where a bank of Princess pine carpets the small rise to my right. Their crisp tendrils, looking up, appear to be the only growing thing I've seen today. [Later, an expert will point out these plants as well as other mosses truly are the only things growing here in winter.]

For a novice map reader my pocket guide is adequate and leaves little room for uncertainty. I leave the blue to try out the yellow trail bumping up against the private land from where I can hear carpenters hammering. I circuit a hill which blocks my view. I know by my breathing I'm climbing a little and the sounds move, first coming from ahead, then to my right and finally disappearing to the rear. No intrusion of traffic here, only workmen's hammers. The land bank has done a good thing isolating these woodlands from further encroachment by our homes and shops.

I walk a short spell on an old lane, grass covered and brown. A few spots of thin mud from the current thaw prove no obstacle and soon there is a view over more stone fences and "Posted" signs beyond in another private nature preserve. Tall oaks and maples seem to me up about fifty to seventy-five feet, their bony fingers still in the morning's breezeless calm. I'm surprised there aren't squirrels dodging Lilly ahead or the sounds of birds except an occasional distant crow's caw-caw. Suddenly I reach a grassy clearing and see two or three poled houses, probably for swallows which can make a dent in the mosquito population. I have friends in West Tisbury who claim there's no such thing in that town. Then comes the final assault to the ridge where I'm bound. The trail is well worn, even with the tracks of an all-terrain bike's tires. Trees are stunted here at the summit. Hot sun and blasting winds must make any growth difficult. In fact, the wind at this elevation is pushing at me now and flapping my open jacket. I've left the quiet day below and I am face to face with Waskosim's Rock, a great beached whale lying on the border between Chilmark and West Tisbury.

From Nan Doty, Education Director in the Wampanoag Tribal Office, and an hour's leafing through the Chilmark section of Charles E. Bank's "History of Martha's Vineyard," I've learned that this great rock probably served as some travel reference as well as a site of ceremonies. In the seventeenth century, at least for a time, a line drawn from the rock, west through the center of the Island to Menemsha Pond, was called the middle line. It connected with another line drawn from Menemsha horizontally (north and south) to Quitsa on the south. As you faced west toward Menemsha Pond everything on the left belonged to the English., everything on the right to the Wampanoags. Thousands of years ago, the last glacier gouged out the earth pushing it ahead, upending layers from below into the irregular ridges and valleys hereabouts. As it quit on its way to the southeast, the glacier lifted this immense rock like a pebble. Here it rests, a reminder of the force which brought it.

A year ago I came here with Alex , my grandson, then nine years old. "Grampa, let's climb the rock." Of course we climbed the rock. Who wouldn't climb the rock on a day with his grandson egging him on? Easy climb it was, up the back side where the giant transverse split provides a slanting foothold and adjacent branches hand support. But the top narrows so that two feet can't be put comfortably apart to balance. My seventy years that day began to betray me. Alex was scrambling like a mountain goat all about the top. "Be careful. I can't carry you all the way back if you fall and break your leg." That was wasted breath of course. We started down, Alex first. As I backed awkwardly and fearfully down my retreat, a young woman wearing a small back pack appeared out of the bushes. "Are you all right? Do you need help to get down?" I imagined that someone had been watching me in some magical way and sent her to the rescue.

"Oh no. I'm OK," I mustered up as much heartiness as I could. She gave me a quizzical look, hesitated, then probably saw in her mind's eye a clumsy effort to aid an old man, and kept on going, didn't even stop to admire the rock. I managed to rejoin Alex none the worse for wear except for an exaggerated feeling, not for the first time, of my own advancing decay.

To the northeast of the great rock is a little rise with a gorgeous view of the ice pond below, the ice house, now with a porch for summer gazing, and down the long flat valley to Vineyard Haven. The water tower off State Road stands alone above the trees and off to the left is the old fire tower at Indian Hill. One sees the tree canopy over a substantial portion of this mid-Island scene. Its uniformity suggests brooms poised to sweep the sky. Colors are black to gray. Hardly a rooftop or clearing breaks the view. As I turn to go back toward the west again, I'm surprised to see a rooftop, closer than I thought possible, probably the site of the carpenter's hammering. I hope they're on the proper side of Waskosim's Rock and the middle line.

The trek back is mostly downhill and this time, on the blue trail, I admire a good length of the Mill Brook as it makes up into a reasonable stream, flowing as I imagine the sweet Afton flows, not with the chattering of Tennyson's babbling brook. The lattice work of superficial trunk roots makes the trail a little uneven and slippery but the pattern's beauty makes up for any inconvenience. A small bridge lifts you up out of the mud in springtime. Lilly begins to sense a return trip and races ahead. We meet a toddler on foot with his dad. Lilly licks the child's face. He won't mind, his father tells me. Used to it.

As I replace my map at the bulletin board, I realize I never thought to look for the cougar. Next time perhaps.

HOW TO GET THERE: Drive one and a half miles on North Road starting at Humphrey's Bakery and Deli on State Road in West Tisbury. North Road junction is just up-island from the bakery. The reservation parking lot is off the road on the south side, (left going up-island) at the Land Bank logo.

Christiantown

Susan Safford

Christiantown

I revisit Christiantown, acquired by the Martha's Vineyard Land Bank in 1986. Thirty years ago I tramped up the dirt road to view the little chapel with my young children. They were particularly intrigued by the burying ground across the way. They were accustomed to the cemetery in Vineyard Haven with its roughly mown grass and orderly tall light-colored grave stones. Many were carved with ornate designs. Carved angels on miniature stones sometimes knelt with folded wings at the graves of children. The death's head frightened the youngest of our crew. Here at Christiantown they had many questions about the moss covered field stones arranged in an order of sorts without the precision of the old cemetery on Centre Street. Why are they buried so close together? Why aren't their names carved? Why doesn't somebody mow the grass? The children learned then about the differences in culture they would find increasingly at issue as they grew older. To this day we accept that the Indian buried his dead in a vertical position resembling the fetal position in the mother's womb.

I peek into the windows of the locked chapel. Spotless freshly painted walls, floors, and pews reflect the light of the gray day admitted by many clear windows. There is no frill or decoration here. I see the black-clad Puritan minister at the plain podium in front and the rough-clad natives facing him, unaccustomed to straight-backed pews, far from their woodland camp fires. Today, a large frond of dried marsh grasses adorns the austere front wall behind the podium and a small wreath of vines hangs at the back inside the door. The chapel is a gem. At the foot of the path leading to the burying ground across the road sits a large boulder with a bronze tablet affixed. It was erected by the

Daughters of the American Revolution "... to commemorate ... The services of Governor Thomas Mayhew / And his descendant missionaries who have labored / Among the native Indians".

My springer, Lilly, is recovering from newly discovered diabetes so the short walk around the one loop trail is just right for her first outing since treatment began. The beech trees are impressive, especially one large clump which has blown over in the wind and erupted a huge seven foot high clod of sandy soil along the trail. The shallow root structure betrays the beech's vulnerability to wind. Leafless woods today uncover an unusual number of blow-downs in this area which seems well protected. Back at the road, we cross over and walk along the several paths up the hillside among the more than 200 graves. The weathered field stones are sitting firmly on edge oriented in the same direction, east and west, except for three far to the north, somewhat separate which are facing at right angles to the rest. Only one that I can see in the whole area is an English style stone made of carved limestone or marble with an inscription. The rest are unmarked. At the top of the small hill an area of springy emerald moss surrounds many of the sites. It is impossible to pass along without kneeling to feel the gentle spring beneath my fingers.

Farther up the road on the right is a drive which leads steeply up hill to the fire tower. Years ago it was poorly maintained and always available for a good climb up rickety wooden-ladder-type stairs. Surmounting the top we could look over much of the Vineyard's tree canopy. On a windy day we climbed quickly back to solid ground fearing the swaying would be our downfall. Today, the tower is said to be the original structure but it appears to have been replaced largely by steel and a stable four-legged standard. Now the whole site is surrounded by a stout steel fence with locked gate. A generator hums over some chore apparently essential for this lonely sentinel in the woods.

I come away from this morning's excursion with more questions than I can answer about the early days of Indian life on Martha's Vineyard and how those people were affected by the invasion of North America by the English. Reading the history of this era in books by W.E. Washburn ("Redman's Land / White Man's Law") and by A.M. Josephy ("The Patriot Chiefs") and by Francis Jennings ("The Invasion of North America") is an exercise in outrage. Yet, our daily life experiences here on the Vineyard with our Indian neighbors and friends are curiously muted. I have never spoken with a Native American about his heritage, his inheritance from the European, his curiosity or HIS outrage. I was caught in a typical white man's slip one day in Leslie's Drug Store. The clerk had handed me one dollar bill too many in change for a purchase and caught herself as I took hold of the bills. She indicated the error and I, of course, gave her back the extra dollar but told her I thought she was an Indian giver, that is, someone who gives a gift and then asks or demands it be given back. "Dr. Hoxsie!" exclaimed an indignant young female voice just to my side waiting for the cashier to be finished with me. I turned with a face already burning a hot crimson to face an old friend and patient from Gay Head (Aquinnah). The moment was saved only by her ready laugh at my discomfort but a small hurt had been created for which I am very sorry.

I call Ryan Malonson in Aquinnah to ask some questions about Christiantown. The Malonsons are very interested in the area and take responsibility for looking after the property. The elder Malonson, Donald, is now Chief of the Wampanoag Tribe in Aquinnah. I've known Ryan since he was a kid. Talking to him on the phone makes that seem a long time ago. Thomas Mayhew brought Christianity to the Indians. Ryan confirms what I have read over time. Christiantown was part of a Takemmy village. The inhabitants moved about a lot. In summers they went south, toward the outwash plain and toward the sea to fish, gather berries, dig clams, and herd their animals. In winter they moved back to Christiantown where the land is sheltered, easier to keep warm. The English gradually moved in and displaced the Indians farther to the west into Menemsha and eventually to Aquinnah or to the south, eventually to Chappaquiddick. I ask Ryan if he thinks any deeds were transferred, money changed hands. He thinks not. The white people just moved in. Ironically the tribe purchased the chapel and burial ground here eight or ten years ago. Hattie Smalley was the last of the Christiantown Indians. She died back in the sixties. Her husband was Amos of white whale fame.

In ancient times there were many villages of Indians on the Vineyard, all Wampanoags. Each had its own identity and individuality, offshoots of the Nobnocket and Takemmy groups. I ask Ryan how he feels about the early christianization of the Indians, the "praying Indians." He replies that some Indians took up the white man's ways, adapted to the English. My mother goes to church; my father doesn't. My white part is Christian. My spiritual part is in the forest. My father says, 'I don't need a cathedral to listen to the Great Spirit.'"

HOW TO GET THERE: Drive up-island on State Road from Vineyard Haven. Bear right on Indian Hill Road just beyond Upper Lambert's Cove Road. Take first right on Christiantown Road and drive 0.6 mile to the chapel on the left where there is parking. The Burial Ground is across from the chapel and the road to the fire tower is 0.1 mile farther on Christiantown Road on the right. The fire tower is closed during the winter.

Sepiessa Point

Ken Vincent

Sepiessa Point

I leave the house after lunch with an eye to the southwest where gray scudding clouds seem to be shouting the announcement of rain. Wind has come up and the gusts are a lungful. Somehow the call to walk is stronger than the clouds' warnings and Lilly, the springer, and I set out for New Lane in West Tisbury and Sepiessa Point. This 164 acre reservation was bought in 1991 by Martha's Vineyard Land Bank. The roads are mostly deserted this winter afternoon. Mild temperatures, the like of which bless the mid Atlantic states this time of year, undermine my age-old sense of being a sturdy New Englander. Water level is low along Tiah's (rhymes with Hiya!) Cove on the white trail. A year and a half ago passage along this trail was blocked by high water at a time of heavy rains. A lone swan stands nervously on the mud flat in front. She is young, still sporting some of the dark feathers of her gosling days. She'll soon be fully grown and white as snow. In a moment when I am out of view she resumes her crouching rest on the mud and crooks her head into her side. A few yards farther I see her mate, swimming in stately leisure. A distant pair of black ducks on the opposite shore are the only other living creatures I see.

As we head inland away from water among the pitch pine woods I hear the undulating drumming of the distant surf. Its deep throated voice calls out to come closer, ever closer. The path is well worn with fresh tracks, even the deeper imprints of horse shoes. There's plenty of room each side in the skimpy brush to retreat if someone canters by. There is nowhere to escape the call of the surf. The white trail joins another and the two travel together toward the shore and its ever-calling roar whose pitch heightens and volume swells. The pines give way to oaks. Oak tops appear as if they have been shaved by a giant razor of wind-driven salt spray sculpting them into a slowly descending arc toward ground level the more closely they grow to the sea.

We come into a clearing through a little side trail at the edge of another narrower cove called Tississa. The local people, my friend Virginia tells me, say simply Tissa. The broad mud flats here are also extensive without the pond water lapping up to the trees as on my last visit. I realize there is probably no tidal rise and fall here in winter if the opening to the sea has closed off. With only light rains and the steady evaporation of water the pond level drops to its present level. Next spring the dunes will be opened to the sea again, admitting the salt water to nourish the life of the pond. Now the trail is high and dry. Twenty thousand years ago the last glacier's melting water ran off toward the south just in this area. The run-off created a series of finger-like projections we now recognize as Tiah's Cove, Deep Bottom Cove, Long Cove, Watcha Pond and Oyster Pond. Tissa, like its nickname, is an abbreviated variety.

The walk so far has been slowed by Lilly's unrelenting interest in the undergrowth and accumulation of leaves along the path. We have stopped two dozen times to let her sniff and rummage. Finally a tug on her leash sets her back on the trail. We finally arrive at the actual point of Sepiessa. The approach is marked by low bushes, recently mowed as part of the land bank's on-going restoration of original native grasses. Whenever grassland is left undisturbed for long enough time, invasion with succession species of trees and bushes inevitably occurs. Historically, recurrent fires and intrusions of salt water preserved these areas. Future walkers well may be able to sight many new species of grasses and wild flowers as well as increased animal life, moles, mice, hawks, and owls.

To my great surprise the beach beyond is broad and long to either side along the Tisbury Great Pond into which both Tissa and Tiah's Coves lead. No wonder I hear so many folks in the summer say what a treat they had swimming at Sepiessa. The wind now is unobstructed and lends another dimension to the sensory stimulus of this particular day. The air rushes past my ears, in fact, blows Lilly's ears straight back along her neck. The roar of the surf and the tactile brushing by of the wind compete to capture my senses.

We are no longer alone. Three brave fishermen in very small boats are on the pond. They carry neither pole nor dredge but are intent on what is below them. We walk along the beach to the west and around the point. Signs tell us these waters are seeded with young shell fish. The weather is really intense here, no season for a gentle swim in the pond. We pass a canoe on the sand and find the entrance to the trails, taking the inland trail back to the car and parking area at the end of Tiah's Cove Road. Now the surf is bidding farewell as it fades perceptibly at our backs. I loosen my jacket and we sit on a log by the side of the trail for a drink of water and a breather. I unleash Lilly and for the rest of the way back she takes on new life scampering back and forth, always in my sight, and seldom stopping to rummage needlessly about.

We've seen the impressive work of restoring the grasslands at the end of Sepiessa Point with the hope of restoring habitat for owls and hawks. We've seen men at work presumably taking care of the young shell fish in the pond and we've seen the source of much pleasure in the opening up of this large tract of shore for both summer and winter activities. This day particularly we've been in touch with the wind and the surf. As we drive back to Chilmark a few large rain drops spatter the windshield and dry as fast as they appear.

HOW TO GET THERE: Start at the intersection of Old County Road and the West Tisbury-Edgartown Road near the center of West Tisbury. Drive toward Edgartown and turn right on New Lane which becomes Tiah's Cove Road. Drive 1.2 miles and park on the left across from the trail head. There are directions for driving to the boat slide at Sepiessa Point or for putting in a canoe in at Tiah's Cove.

Tisbury Meadow   Ken Vincent

Tisbury Meadow

Winter has arrived in January finally. This morning my window thermometer reads 7 degrees Fahrenheit and the air outside is crystal clear. By nine the temperature is up ten degrees and a sense of adventure commands me to get out in the great outdoors and test my mettle against tardy Jack Frost. Lilly, the springer, is always game. In fact, some evenings when the wife and I have advanced the thermostat a bit to take the chill away, Lilly barks to go out and for a half hour or more will sit quietly watching the driveway in the dark, cooling her underside on the crispy grass by the back steps. I'm bundled up today and we arrive at the trail-head for Tisbury Meadow with thin sunshine streaming from the south. We've all seen the lovely meadow along the southern edge of State Road on the way out of Tisbury past Lower Lambert's Cove Road. Years ago it was called Mai Fain's Fields, a huge sloping green to run through or amble along on its paths. If I have a mind to, I can notice the cars going by and wave to a familiar driver. Mostly I have eyes on my footing and the bits of ice and frozen snow patches which may upset the apple cart on this crisp morning. The area offers much more than meets the eye. The meadow is the showcase and we soon complete the circle around its circumference and meet up with the trail to the woods. It is part of an 83 acre preserve maintained by Martha's Vineyard Land Bank. From here one can mount a more ambitious walk to nearby Ripley's Field, Wompesket and Cranberry Acres over Red Coat Hill Road or to Stony Hill Road to the west on Old Holmes Hole Road or to Wapatequa Woods via Old Holmes Hole Road. This morning I elect to explore the southern stretches toward Old Holmes Hole Road and back toward Nobnocket

We take the yellow trail which soon gives onto the red and into the woods. I'm grateful for the sun, thin as it seems this time of year, streaming in through the bare tree branches. The way is up and over the esker (a glacially formed ridge). A lone crow wings his way through the woods. I wonder how he can avoid all the obstructions in his flight, the trunks and branches at all angles and distances. I've never seen a crow collide with a tree. His navigational equipment is superb. The woods here provide a shelter from the southwest wind and the sun in my face is comfortable, erasing the frigid wind of the open meadow. Another yellow trail takes off to the left and soon we come to an ancient rutted road, Old Holmes Hole Road. It looks to me that the old Vineyarders took one of two paths up or down-island to avoid the high ridge or esker. Initially they came more southward on this ancient way. Later, for some reason, perhaps to hook up better with Lambert's Cove or to reach the fresh water at Tashmoo, they took the current route of State Road down the hill past Craig Kingsbury and up to Nobnocket. In several places the ancient road comes into a deep depression which fills easily with water. Today these little ponds are frozen but don't look quite safe enough to traverse on foot. There is a ready-made solution in every case, an alternate path, high and dry, obviously not so old, skirting the little pond and rejoining the road beyond. The way a cow meanders describes aptly these circuitous paths which keep one's feet dry or a wagon from becoming mired in the mud.

Soon after we leave the land bank's preserve the road becomes more finished and wider. Soon we are surrounded by commercial and residential buildings, a tar road replaces the dirt and I can see ahead familiar buildings on the far side of State Road above the Tashmoo look-out. The walk back along State Road is uncomfortable next to the steady traffic down-Island. The verge is narrow and uneven. I keep Lilly on a short leash.

None of the drivers returns my wave. They're probably thinking it's too cold a day for a man and his dog to be walking along
State Road. Now the sun is hidden behind the buildings and ele-
vated land on my left. If I had thought the weather was moder-
ating with the sun in my face before, I am brought up short to
how really chilly the morning remains. I am more self conscious
than ever now, as I draw up my scarf over my cold runny nose
and avert my eyes from the passing drivers.

Perhaps the sudden change in weather has started me thinking about ice and snow. In fact, I find myself in front of my
warm Vermont Castings stove poring through an old
Encyclopedia Britannica to find out more about eskers. The
word esker (from the old Irish, eiscar) has been burning in my
mind since the walk at Brightwood Park in Tisbury. Volume 8
of the E.C. tells me an esker is a long, often winding, ridge of
layered gravel and sand in regions of former glaciation. It represents material formerly filling the channels of streams under,
within or even upon the ice. The material is left behind when the
ice melts. Now I can imagine a rapid stream running along as the
brook runs from my childhood swimming hole. In the shallows
the stream stirs up ripples on the bottom, gradually building up
material into significant ridges. The heavier the flow of water
the higher these ridges become. Well, that's interesting but it's
just the beginning.

Soon I am learning more than the editor will possibly accept
for my article about Tisbury Meadow but some of it contains
answers to questions I've asked about glaciers for a long time
and I plow ahead to Volume 9. Glaciers originate as a body of
ice on land by compaction and recrystallization of snow and ice
and show evidence of movement. They form when the annual
snow fall exceeds the melting in the summer and exist in modern times on earth in high mountains and the polar regions.
They occupy 10 percent of the earth's surface. Ninety-six per-

cent are found in Antarctica and Greenland, the remainder scattered over all continents except Australia. They contain enough ice to mantle the earth 100 to 200 feet thick. If all the existing ice melted, the sea level would rise 200 feet and submerge every coastal city in the world. Antarctic ice can be up to 8000 feet thick As the glacier forms, tremendous pressure is exerted on the lowest levels of solid ice and the ice is changed in physical character enabling it to flow as cold molasses. When the weight of the ice becomes so great as to overcome the strength of the ice below to hold it, the body of ice begins to move with the flow of the lowest levels of "molasses" ice. As the glacier descends below the snow line it begins to melt and form run-off streams. When it reaches ocean, hunks of ice break off and float away as ice bergs. As the surface of the glacier becomes unstable from the movement, ice cracks, producing great crevasses.

The maximum velocity of movement of a glacier has been recorded at 150 feet per day but the typical movement is more like a few inches or a few feet per day. The movement acts at the lowest levels like a giant rasp or sand paper. Great rocks and tons of gravel and earth are pushed along by the glacier often turning under layers of sand and clay as they have done at the Gay Head cliffs. At the glacial terminus, ice melts and deposits its random collection in mounds and ridges as terminal moraines like those at Felix Neck and along the hills of Chilmark. Drumlins are clusters of elongated hills oriented parallel to the direction of ice movement laid down at the edges of the glacier. As ice melts the material laid down is reworked by melt-water streams building outwash plains and terraces. Kettles are depressions in the outwash plain formed by blocks of ice buried deep in the outwash deposit. Eskers are the winding ridges of stratified gravel deposited by outwash streams.

So I am back to eskers. My adventure in the cold of this tardy winter season has spawned, not only a surge in my energy and delight in cold weather once more but also has driven me to answer some old incompletely answered questions, thanks to Tisbury Meadow and Britannica.

HOW TO GET THERE: Drive up-island on State Rd from Vineyard Haven to Tashmoo Overlook. Go 0.4 mi farther and turn into the 3rd driveway on the left past Lower Lambert's Cove Road at land bank sign. Parking is in the rear. The map at trail head and the latest 'Land Bank Public Lands Map' are best to show the relationship of Tisbury Meadow, the other preserves mentioned and several ancient ways. The meadow walk is about 1.0 mi; the Wompesket walk is 3.5 - 4.0 miles; the walk on Holmes Hole Road to Nobnocket and back is 3.0 miles.

Long Point

Ken Vincent

Long Point Wildlife Refuge

Rafe Teller and I make a date to walk Long Point Wildlife Refuge, a huge 633 acre preserve acquired in 1979 by The Trustees of Reservations. This morning's temperature is 30 degrees, wind gusting and wind chill probably close to 10 above. We are bundled up well and drive down Deep Bottom Road, a mile west of the airport. For this late in the winter the road is in pretty good repair with frequent turn-outs if we should meet some one else but we don't see another soul along the two and a half miles to the parking lot. We've been to this small lot before, now used only for off-season parking. A much larger lot inside the dunes at the shore is available in summer on another road. That's another story for later.

I tell Rafe that I scouted out the approach here two weeks ago with Lilly but kept seeing signs saying "No Dogs Allowed". I thought I might be sneaky and walk with her nevertheless but the last sign dissuaded me. "No Dogs Beyond This Point Any Time of Year". Lilly and I retreated then for another walk at another location. She stays home today. I am about to burden Rafe with a diatribe about the Trustees of Reservations being pet-unfriendly when I spy another sign just beyond the parking. It explains the No Dog signs. This whole area is a breeding ground for many wild species, including hawks, eagles, plovers and others. Even good dogs, properly leashed, says the sign, will look like predators to the wild things which may desert the area entirely if frightened. I wonder if someone has studied the effect on eagles and hawks of a very polite leashed springer spaniel but I keep that thought to myself.

We settle down to enjoy this brisk morning. Soon we are both drawing up collars around our necks and chins. As we leave the wooded area toward the beach, the southwest wind blasts at us with fury. My cheeks begin to feel numb. We have thoughts of turning back but something about the air, the clear air, the grassy plain ahead, draws us onward. Any wild thing taking refuge here today is playing smart, smarter than we I judge. We see nothing of animal or bird life stirring. I turn around to take a quick breather from the wind and realize we are now standing in an immense grassy plain. Its dull wheat color, briskly waving grass and uniform texture are spectacular. Behind us stand the wind-sculpted oak and a few stunted pitch pines. Ahead we see the low dunes and hear the roar of the ocean. Roped-off areas keep us off rehabilitation projects for natural grasses here and in the dunes. We come to a break in the dunes soon enough. Through the narrow opening the deep blue of the sea and, then, the foaming breakers striking the long beach from Edgartown to Squibnocket take our breath away. The wind is nothing at this moment compared to the visual effect through the dune opening. Sand blows down the beach. We can barely hear ourselves talk and we stand transfixed for a few wonderful moments looking to the south where we see nothing but broad blue ocean; to the west, the nearby frozen surface of Tisbury Great Pond and, farther, the orangy cliffs at Vincent's Beach and Squibnocket while in back of us, this vast grassy plain.

We head back now to the east along the shore of Long Cove Pond. A break in the brush as we regain the stunted wooded area brings us to the very edge of the pond. The frozen opaque surface, powdery blue mixed with tans and grays lies stark against the after image of that bright blue beyond the dunes. The roar of the surf here in the lee is a distant hum; the wind seems to have disappeared. Rafe notices a picnic table nearby. "We could sit down to have our lunch if we'd brought lunch," he says. It seems warm enough certainly.

The difference in the Vineyard landscape between summer and winter is remarkable. Visitors who have seen the Vineyard only in summer are amazed to find the change. "Look how far you can see into the woods now," they say. My previous visits here were always in the summer on the search for a beach and salt water. Today is a revelation for me as well. Back near the parking lot we follow the signs for the Middle Cove loop. It is the topper for our walk today. We are at the edge of a small cove, more closely framed than any of the other vistas we've been enjoying. The short brush and few pine branches framing our side of the pond give out to the quiet ice of the surface and, beyond on the far shore, oak woods, perfectly uniform, bent by the wind and salt, trunks and branches gray and ghostly reaching up to the partly clouded sky. Rafe points his camera and shoots the scene. How soon would we come across these exact conditions again?

I am puzzled by the reference to "summer" parking. We peruse our maps to see just where it might be. The next day I learn from a friend who has been coming to Long Point all her life that we have come today the "old way": down Deep Bottom Road, then sharply to the left (east) on Watcha Road, then sharply right on Long Point Road. Summer Parking is farther to the east on Waldon's Bottom Road. We leave Long Point, retracing our route in the red pick-up and turn on another road leading east. What I haven't figured on are the huge puddles now frozen in this poorly maintained road. I am soon stranded in the middle of a small lagoon, having broken through ice with a menacing slosh and jounce. Luck is with us today. The four wheel drive functions superbly and, in reverse, I navigate by rear-view mirror out of the broken ice. The narrow road and thick bushes on either side prohibit even the thought of turning around. Rafe navigates from the passenger seat and I reverse our way back to reconnect with my friend's "old way." Soon we're driving toward West Tisbury and Chilmark on tarmac. "Enough exploration for one day, Rafe," I say. "We'll find "Summer Parking" another time.

HOW TO GET THERE: Off-Season - From the junction with Barnes Road, drive 1.1 miles toward West Tisbury on W. T.-Edgartown Rd. Turn left on Deep Bottom Rd. at the Long Point sign. Drive two and a half miles following Long Point signs to parking area. Map at trail head shows the trails and points of interest. Summer - Drive toward West Tisbury on W. T. Tisbury Edgartown Road to the entrance to M.V. Airport. Turn almost immediately left onto Waldon's Bottom Road. Follow Long Point signs for the nearly 2 miles distance to parking.

Cape Poge Light   Betsy Corsiglia

North Neck Highland Preserve

How do I get to Chappy early enough to watch the sun come up over North Neck? I call Curry Jones to find out when the ferry starts to run. "Seven o'clock," he replies. "I'll never make it," I say. "Sun-up is at three minutes before seven." To make short of it, Curry invites to me to stay the night with him and Peggy. What is all this rising at the crack of dawn about anyhow? Research these days indicates that most brain function is chemical-dependent. My brain seems to function all too frequently on simple association. The fourth week in November this year produced a concurrence of new moon and Venus in the southwest sky which was lovely. The moon, a mere 240,000 miles from Earth and Venus, all of 65 and a half million miles away, appeared almost to touch each other. I watched the two separate over the three evenings following. The sight was spectacular. Heavens were dark, but clear and I stood by my back porch and watched until the chill drove me inside. I'm certain this experience has primed me for thinking about the heavens and seeing the dawn in this particularly bright period of weather.

My clock is set for five-thirty and, as usual, I wake a couple of hours early anticipating the inevitable. What is singing in my head as I drift back to sleep? The old song I haven't sung or played on the piano for more than fifty years; "On the road to Mandelay / Where the flying fishes play / And the dawn comes up like thunder / Out of China 'cross the bay." My brain is having a time this week with associations both old and new.

We rise at 5:30, eat a breakfast of fresh-laid eggs, scrambled with Spam (haven't had that since the Army) and we set out for the Land Bank Preserve between the gut and Cape Pogue Pond. Curry and I drive to the park area at North Neck and slowly climb the sloped grassy path toward the Edgartown Harbor side of the preserve. Every few steps we pause to look back into the southeast sky. Bright pink spreads like jam across the horizon with layers of yellow and blue. The sky above is gray and dark, cloudless. Gradually the back-light illuminates a low ragged outline of a distant island. Must be Nantucket I think. As we resume our climb the dark clouds hanging over Edgartown take on here and there a faint pink and blue themselves and windows along the shore of the harbor seem almost on fire with reflected eastern light. The familiar church towers hove into view. "That water tower sure does overpower everything else," says Curry. We comment on the controversy that accompanied the original building of that stand.

We reach a solid platform looking out over 360 degrees of unobstructed view. Toward the north we see the lights along the shore at East Chop and the faint image of West Chop light. More to the east hangs Cape Cod. In back of us toward the brightening sky sits the Cape Pogue light. The cape's long elbow travels down toward where we watch, nearly closing off the "gut", that narrow opening into and out of Cape Pogue Pond. I have an acquaintance who thought swimming across it would be easy. Fortunately his companion was a better swimmer and hauled him out of the swift current to shore.

Wherever I watch the sun come up I sense a certain tension, an expectancy of a miracle perhaps. It is true this morning. The sun is not actually rising in the east; we are spinning toward it. The still chill air is surprisingly comfortable. The walk has sped up our circulation. I ask Curry how he can manage without gloves. "An old friend told me once," he says, "if you keep a wool hat pulled down around your ears your hands will stay warm." The emerging ball of fire at the far reach of the ocean bursts on the scene with a blinding yellow light obscuring all that it had back-lit before. We need to look away but we've seen what we came to find.

As the light brightens, the noise of a motor advances from the harbor. A scalloper, the first, sets sight on the gut and the pond. Soon two or three others join the parade. By this time we have descended the steep stairs to the beach and wave to the fishermen. The beach is narrow at the base of surprisingly steep cliffs of sand. This area is actually a narrow rise between the waters of Cape Pogue Pond and Edgartown Harbor where the water issues from the pond. On the pond side we walk along the stony beach wondering if the large rounded stones arranged almost in lines vertical to the shore have been placed here by human hands. "Great Indian country," Curry observes. "Peggy has found arrow heads here," he says, pointing to the base of the sand cliff. "I've never found one myself."

"My wife has the same experience when she walks the beaches at Aquinnah, I respond with a shake of my head. "I've never found one either." "The pond is very shallow," Curry says, "and high winds whip up some mighty waves." On this calm morning it's hard to believe that a boat might be endangered here. "Just so," says my friend.

Part of this area is owned and maintained by the Edgartown Preservation Society. Between the land bank and the town, the public has access to two interesting beaches and great fishing, Curry tells me. "You, know, don't you, that Edgartown has 60 per cent of the available beaches on the Vineyard." He harrumphs a little, alluding to "you up-islanders who keep most of your beaches to yourselves."

I think this site on Chappaquiddick is little known to most Vineyarders except, of course, Chappy residents and serious fishermen. I return home for a little extra shut-eye thinking I have been too long discovering this particular spot. The thunderous sunrise "out of China 'cross the bay" can have nothing on the one we've seen this morning out of Nantucket 'cross the sound.

HOW TO GET THERE: From the Chappaquiddick ferry, drive 1.3 miles and turn left on North Neck Road. Drive another 1.3 miles and park at the land bank lot which is marked. Walk north up the slight hill to the stairway to the beach and explore the area across from the gut where the fishing is said to be excellent. Drive farther to the second land bank lot and walk to the pond side and walk along the beach there.

Old Sailor's Burial Ground   Ralph Stewart

Old Sailor's Burial Ground

We are walking this still January morning from Tisbury
Meadow Preserve, a Martha's Vineyard Land Bank Commission
property, on a search for the Old Sailor's Burial Ground. I have
skirted about it on a couple of occasions walking along Old
Holmes Hole Road (OHHR), one of the many ancient ways in
Tisbury and Oak Bluffs. My springer spaniel, Lilly, seems to
have taken on new life with medicine both for diabetes and
arthritis. My wife sends us off with a caution not to walk too far.
Recent snow melting and refreezing has left the trails rough and
slippery. I'll do well not to break a hip clambering up and over
the glacial esker found in this region. Lilly is beside herself and
finds, then buries, a deer leg, by the look and smell of it left by
a recent hunter. OHHR begins to look familiar as I turn left on
its wider expanse and modestly traveled surface. The maps and
my sense of direction are little more than useless because of the
many intersecting foot and cart paths. Some are well traveled, a
few even boast an untrodden snow cover.

I take the first right turn off OHHR and follow my nose
always pushing toward the left sensing I'll soon be closer to
town where a cemetery most likely will lie. This bit of instinctu-
al wisdom will be tested sorely a little later. We come to another intersection and I am stumped except for the almost immediate appearance from the road to my left of George Fisher in his
shiny white Oak Bluffs police cruiser. "Just the man I could be
looking for," I say with some relief. To make it short I have
actually come to Burial Ground Road and George is going home
for something he must have forgotten. "Just follow the road I've
come along for a quarter mile and you'll see the gate posts," he
tells me.

Two stubby field-stone posts joined by a sturdy chain mark the entrance to the "Historic Seaman's Friend Society Cemetery". A large wooden sign adds that it is managed by the Boston Seaman's Friend Society, first burial occurring in 1888. On a slight rise sits an almost square fenced-in field with short wild grass covered with snow and many tall straight middle-aged oaks. Obviously someone has been cleaning up this place for a while. The adjoining field is a mass of tangled grass and brush. At the extremity of the lot at the top of the rise three or four irregular rows of cement markers are the only evidence aside from the sign that this place is resting ground for 72 unnamed sailors. The markers are uniform, similar to surveyor's bounds and each is surmounted by a number fashioned of dull stout zinc or lead wire stapled in place. One or two numbers are missing and the last two graves in the second row retain a thick wooden slab as marker in addition. One lies flat, broken at ground level, the other firmly anchored in the earth. I walk down each line following another set of footsteps in the snow. The back row takes a jog downhill to make a place for the oak which must have predated the marker. An eerie feeling follows me as I return to the road - all these men buried without fanfare, without name or date, on the outskirts of town under circum-stances little understood. Two modern cape cottages occupy spaces across the road, recent intrusions into the woods of a town expanding much beyond its limits of the nineteenth centu-ry. All the other ancient cemeteries are within the town - behind Association Hall in Vineyard Haven, on the hill overlooking the harbor off Delano Road and at Grove Avenue toward West Chop. I am standing today in what once must have been a very lonely place. Lilly and I return quietly, maneuvering around the now more slippery ice with the added melt of the day's noon-time warmth, my mind immersed in the past.

Back at home, still affected by the poignancy, the desolation, the sadness of what I have seen, I look at my few notes. The telephone numbers from the cemetery sign give me the hope of bringing some human dimension to the benighted plot of ground on the outskirts of Vineyard Haven. A local call lands me an appointment with Shawn Ahearn, manager of the Vineyard branch of Boston Seaman's Friend Society housed in the old DAR Building on Main Street, Vineyard Haven. Among the relics he cares for is an old Bible listing some of the names of those buried in the lot I saw the day before. Shawn surmises that the burial of at least some of the sailors so far from the center of town and other burial sites was dictated by the infectious nature of their terminal illnesses - small pox, consumption (TB), dysentery. This was certainly a custom in the 18th and 19th centuries when the exact nature of contagion was little understood. All over New England one can find isolated small grave yards or single graves in out-of-the-way places, their occupants sequestered from the larger society for its supposed protection.

I call Ted Coates, director of the renamed Boston Seafarer's Friend Society. He tells me about a book by George William Wiseman called "They Kept the Lower Lights Burning," inspired by the long chaplaincies of Madison Edwards and his son-in-law, Austin Tower, at the Seaman's Bethel, an arm of the Society, in Vineyard Haven. It specifically cites the seamen who lie in Vineyard ground. Many died at the Marine Hospital, their names: Delgarde, Hanson, Loderburg, Walruth, McDonald, Alley, Chevaria; their homes often distant: Cape Verde, Maine, Norway, Finland, Holland, Germany, Alabama, Spain. Many have a simple entry "Name Unknown, Washed Ashore."

"That burial ground "is one of the saddest things there is," Coates tells me. "We're going to try to set up a monument to honor them and hold a memorial service to dedicate it to their memory. I think we can even place the names on the internet for people out there searching family records of lost loved ones whose whereabouts have never been determined."

I talk with Allan Wilson, chair of the Vineyard Advisory Committee to the Seafarer's Friend Society. He acknowledges the long period of acrimony which has existed at least since the 1960's between the Town of Tisbury and the society after the society had bought both the old decommissioned Marine Hospital and its accompanying burial ground in 1956. Disagreement over the use of a large bequest by Harriet Goldberg to the Seaman's Bethel for benefit of island seafarers' families and local outrage at the neglect of the burial ground seems to have been settled after a lengthy court battle. In addition to plans for the burial ground, the society now provides money to seafaring families on the Vineyard in the form of scholarship aid to their children or to any high school graduate who wishes to pursue a career on the sea. In the past three years Mr. Wilson estimates about 10 to 12 thousand dollars in scholarship awards have been made and $8000 in new scholarships for next year plus $18,000 in renewed scholarships for those already having received a first year's grant. He hopes that the future will see annual awards of 6 to 8 thousand dollars each year in addition to renewing previous grants as long as the student remains in school. One grant of $25,000 to Habitat for Humanity was made in 1999.

Obviously Vineyard seafarers and the old cemetery have been forgotten for a long time but people at present are beginning to remember. My walk this week has been more than exercise for a man and his dog. More likely it has been balm to his modern spirit, often overcome by cynicism and lack of faith in fellow humans.

HOW TO GET THERE: For a comfortable walk, better without snow and ice on the ground, drive up-island on State Road in Vineyard Haven to the third driveway on the left past Lower Lambert's Cove Road and turn into the parking area at Tisbury Meadow Preserve. Take the white trail to Old Holmes Hole Road (OHHR) and turn left. You will have passed the bound for the land bank property but the trail continues to the road. At the first junction leave OHHR on the right and take either the foot path to your left or the cart track on your right. Each brings you to Burial Ground Road (unmarked). Turn left for one-quarter to half a mile for the Burial Grounds on your left. An easier way is to take Canterbury Lane on the right off Edgartown Road just in-town from the Senior Citizen's Apartments. Turn right at the T. Before the cul-de-sac turn left on Burial Ground (dirt) Road to the area. This ancient way passes close to private property. Be careful to observe no trespassing signs and private driveways.

Tick Drag - Cedar Tree Neck   Ralph Stewart

Tick Drag - Cedar Tree Neck

Come along today while I indulge in some fun with the word drag. In 1955 at Shirley Frisch's Halloween costume party, I dressed in drag and wondered ever since what my newly met friends thought. For several month's in the 1970's my oldest son went drag racing but, to his parent's great relief, thought better of it as he grew older. And to get one-up on a competitor or a better table at an expensive restaurant, some people pull drag. Jim Morgan, in the waters off the Vineyard drags for flounder and yellowtails[1]. Last week my grandson, Alex, said, "Going back to school is a drag." This week I've gone dragging for ticks with Barnstable County entymologist Dave Simser at Cedar Tree Neck, a Sheriff's Meadow Sanctuary in West Tisbury. The latter is becoming my frequent walking place. This trip we walked in 30 second increments as reading further will make clear.

Dave and I arrive at Cedar Tree Neck under dark gray skies and threatening rain drops. "Wet will not be good for today," Dave says and his remark seems to hold off a downpour as he pulls out a green fly rod case and begins to withdraw an unlikely looking fishing pole. It is a 4 foot rod on which is attached a half meter square flannel, fuzzy on both sides. "My Aunt Julie stitched up the sides," he says. I think it is a little grungy and he remarks that it is never washed for fear of contaminating it with soap offensive to ticks. "When I finish with it each day I put it through the dryer at home to kill any tick larvae." These tiniest of tick forms apparently may cover the flannel during drags in the early season. [This is a good tip for treating clothes worn through tick country to be sure they are tick-free.] Pointing to

1 Oral History of Jimmy Morgan...as told to Linsey Lee,
VINEYARD Style, Holiday 2001.

the ground, Dave says, "Tick nymphs [slightly larger after molting from larval forms] hunker down here looking for mice hosts. [Larger] adult forms climb taller grass hunting deer." He is dragging or waving the flannel sheet on his pole along the trail over brush and leaves and grass, counting 1000-one, 1000-two and so on for 30 seconds, then stops to examine the sheet and count ticks. He points to two or three females. "Telling males from females becomes easy; males are smaller," he says. "After you've done this a while they are obvious and if you find dog ticks they look like elephants. Here, you take a turn."

So I walk along and mimic his action except I'm caught for an instant in a green-briar. "Aha!" he says. "You're a natural." It's not rocket science I think. I get 3 or 4 more female adults on my sheet. Next Dave demonstrates the tiny vials for tick collection. First he stretches a tiny square of latex non-powdered glove material over the top and secures it with a snap-on rim. The vials have water moistened plaster of Paris in the bottom for humidity. Then he punctures the latex with fine tipped tweezers and grasps one of my ticks by her red abdomen and gently inserts her through the tiny hole and withdraws the forceps. "There's a pinged tick," he says with some exultation. "The trouble with the smaller nymphs is that they sometimes get caught just at the opening of the hole like on a tiny drum top and ping right up into my face, not nice." "Oh man!" I exclaim.

Now it's my turn. The forceps are delicate and the tick tiny. I manage after a couple of tries to puncture the cap but rip it wide. Now the ticks inside can escape. Obviously I need practice. "Pitfalls of ticking," Dave says, "Plus mosquitoes and deer flies in summer. You're holding the vial in one hand, the drag under your arm, trying to ping the tick through the cap with the other and swat flies all at once. Stabbing yourself in the eye is a distinct danger." He goes on to say that this little stretch of trail right off the parking area always yields ticks and after a couple

more 30-second walks, he counts out our total: 3 boys and 7
girls, all adults. Considering we've done only four stretches of
trail for 30 seconds apiece that's 300 ticks per hour. Actually our
visit today is a simple survey to see if there are ticks here at all
in this season. A full round of dragging is forty 30-second drags.
We'll discard these and Dave starts to toss our collection into
the brush. "I send these guys back to nature," he says. "The rule
is that any I find on me die. Later in the summer I'll find common dog ticks, sometimes a brown dog tick and once at
Nickerson Park on Cape Cod I found a lone star tick. The
female has a large spot like a star on its abdomen. I've even
found an assassin bug nymph and occasional pine aphid."

Dave goes on to explain that after finishing an official drag
he would replace the vial cover latex with fine mesh gauze to
keep the ticks from suffocating, collect all the vials from his
drags over a couple of weeks in plastic envelopes with a moistened paper towel inside, then ship them to University of Rhode
Island where the live ticks are assayed for Lyme Disease spirochetes [bacteria]. "They'll live almost indefinitely under these
conditions," he says. "At the lab the ticks are dusted with a
chemical reagent which causes the bacteria within the tick's gut
to fluoresce or give off a yellow color which is visible in ultra-
violet light when viewed under a microscope, a process called
indirect fluoroscopic assay [IFA] or dark-field photography.
When we multiply the number of ticks per hour by the percent
of ticks found positive for the bacteria we get a risk index. This
makes possible an estimated risk of tick exposure in a given
area."

I ask Dave to describe the habits and life cycle of deer ticks.

"Let's start with this season," he begins. "There are two
overlapping generations. One is the population of flat (unfed)
nymphs which are over-wintering and inactive right now [late
February] under the leaf litter on the woods floor. They'll

become aggressive blood seekers from May into July, making Lyme Disease prevalence during this time the highest of the year. By October they will have molted to adults, then feed on deer and begin over-wintering, mating and nourishing fertilized eggs while on deer. In May next year they will lay eggs. New generation larvae will appear in June. By August they will have fed on mice which may be infected with Lyme Disease, then molt and pass any infection on to nymphs who will not feed until after wintering over. The next May they will exit the leaf litter on the woods floor, become active and repeat the cycle. The adults we've found today are unfed and still looking for deer. Lucky ones among them have found a deer, taken a blood meal, laid their eggs on the ground and died. These adults will disappear by April."

"How do you know they die?" I ask. He tells me that you never find unfed adults in summer and lab research under controlled conditions shows deer ticks live only a year in the tropics and no more than two years in temperate zones. No matter how many times I hear this genealogy, I always learn something new with its retelling.

This summer Simser is working on a project with a grant from the Center for Disease Control (CDC) to the Massachusetts Department of Health with cooperation from University of Massachusetts and University of Rhode Island. Using a graduate student's help this summer, he plans to trap rodents (mice, voles, moles, rabbits, and squirrels), taking blood samples and looking for spirochetes of Lyme Disease. The common wisdom tells us that white footed mice are primary hosts of Lyme Disease. If this is true, the other part of the project, establishing bait stations where mice will acquire a coating of an insecticide to kill their attached deer ticks, may be quite successful in reducing wild Lyme Disease. If other rodents are also significant hosts, alternate measures may need to be designed for reduction of rodent infection.

My two visits with David over the last month have renewed my interest in the mysteries of Lyme Disease and my long-time ambition of "trapping" ticks has now been achieved and in the process I have learned a new use for the word drag.

HOW TO GET THERE: Drive up-island on State Road to Indian Hill Road just beyond Upper Lambert's Cove Road in West Tisbury. At 1.7 miles turn right on Daggett Road. Drive on steep bumpy road 1.0 mile to the end. Watch for Sanctuary signs along the way.

Martin House

Grace Church

Great Rock Bight

Julian K. Robinson

African American Heritage Trail

"Where were all the black people then?" the second grade girl asks during Elaine Weintraub's community history project at the Oak Bluffs School in 1989. "There weren't any here then," another girl says before Ms. Weintraub can reply. As she ruminates about the answer, this history teacher, former Paul Cuffe Fellow and Anti-Defamation League award winner, thinks something is amiss. Her painstaking research that follows this tiny incident leads her and collaborator, Mrs. Carrie Tankard, Vice President and Archivist of the Martha's Vineyard Chapter of the NAACP, to a greater understanding of the African-American presence on the Vineyard from earliest colonial times to the present. The fruit of the process is the African American Heritage Trail described in detail in the book of the same name by Weintraub and Tankard and beautifully illustrated in "Vineyard Style" by John Budris and Charlie Utz, Fall and Holiday editions, 2000. I start to explore the trail, not on foot alone since that requires a full circuit of the island, and note that February's Black History Month has become an annual time for recognizing the contribution of African Americans to the fabric of their often cruelly adoptive land. I am not prepared for the discoveries along the way as I revisit the bronze plaque at Great Bight Preserve off North Road in Chilmark near the home of Rebecca, "woman of Africa."

Rebecca endures the cruel Middle Passage from Guinea in West Africa and is sold to Colonel Cornelius Bassett in Chilmark. She marries Elisha Amos, an "Indian man", also named Janoxett, and inherits his farm on the field at Great Bight when he dies. Amos has acquired considerable land including farms at Roaring Brook off North Road and at "the Gay Head" but it changes hands frequently after his death and much of it passes to the Harris family in 1872 who work the land until 1997. In 1779, on the death of Colonel Bassett, Rebecca's daughter, Nancy, 7, and son, Pero, 18, are sold to Joseph Allen of Tisbury but Rebecca remains at the farm, probably a freed woman on the great field until her death in 1801. Before I leave the plaque I am intrigued by the innumerable stones - white, gray, lavender, speckled, spotted, inlaid and streaked - left on the ground about the base of the plaque's boulder. Colorful sankofas, fashioned of one continuous strand of wire, covered with clay and yarns of tans, yellows, reds and blues, are draped about the plaque. They symbolize "the unity of past, present and future."

Ms. Weintraub tells me she gradually uncovers more and more of "a good story" exploring land sales, census tracts and other boring documents. Once in a while she strikes gold. Rebecca's daughter, Nancy, becomes a legend as Black Nance, a fearsome seer often observed in Edgartown shaking her fingers in a frenzy at passers-by after the loss of a sailor at sea. She lives a long, tortured life, ending as a pauper in a small rest home with four or five other souls in similar condition. Her daughter named Rebecca Michael produces a son, William Martin, and, here, Ms. Weintraub begins to mine the more recent past. Martin becomes the whaling captain she has heard rumors about during her research.

I set out with my grandson, Alex, for Chappaquiddick to find the captain's old home and grave. Driving up Jeffers Lane to the hill top we come to the neatly trimmed Chappy graveyard and, at the back, turned away from the magnificent view of Cape Pogue Pond and Nantucket Sound to the south, is Martin's chiseled rock stone - Capt. William A. Martin, July 17, 1830 - September 5, 1907...

Across the road we enter a little-used private drive for a glimpse of the Martin's old home, now owned by others. Its simplicity and shabbiness lie in stark contrast to the magnificent facades of old captain's houses on the Edgartown waterfront, barely a mile away. The great grandson of "woman of Africa" attains the greatness of the Edgartown great but remains separated still from the larger community. Ms. Weintraub thinks that his headstone facing away from the sea, in distinction to the other stones in the yard, indicates his color has defined him for the people of his time.

Twelve-year-old Alex provides an interesting parenthesis to the drive back to the ferry. "We've had a big fight at home about renaming our athletic teams from the Scarborough [Me.] Redskins to The Red Storm," he says. His sentiments against the change are clear to me.

"Well, how would you feel if the name had been changed to The Whiteskins?"

"No problem," he replies. "I don't see why it matters much."

"What does the expression Redskins mean to you, Alex?"

"War paint and bear grease Indians used to spread on their skin to keep warm."

"How would you feel if people remembered your great grandfather because he used war paint and bear grease?"

"It shows the Indians were resourceful, used what they had."

I began to get a picture of how a twelve-year-old takes in impressions.

"Times change; it's past history. Why not forget it," Alex offers.

"I see how you feel," I said, worried now I might soon begin to preach.

On a previous visit to Pecoy Point in Oak Bluffs, I see my first Heritage plaque, the one honoring John Saunders, African-American slave, brought to the Vineyard hidden beneath a load of corn in a schooner's hold. He preaches to people of color living at Farm Neck from atop a giant boulder and brings Methodism to the Vineyard. Madison Edwards, Chaplain of the Seaman's Bethel in Vineyard Haven, invites him to preach at the Oak Bluffs Camp Grounds. Ironically a black preacher can sermonize but blacks are not admitted to the old camp meetings during Saunders's lifetime. The report that Saunders actually speaks to gatherings from the rock strikes me as overly imaginative but, as I clamber up its moss covered side off Pulpit Rock Road across from the westerly drive into Meadow View Farms on County Road, Oak Bluffs, I catch my breath and then spread my arms in the fashion I suspect an energetic preacher might assume. As I utter a few spontaneous words of greeting I become a believer in the story of the rock.

My last visit on the trail takes me to Carrie Tankard in the Oak Bluffs Highlands. She escorts me a short way to the east through the entrance to the old Baptist Temple Park, site of an old tabernacle, marked only by concrete footings of a structure which burned. I now understand the answer to a question an acquaintance put to me the previous week, "Do you know where the Black Tabernacle was?" Carrie tells me this area over many years has been traditional home in summer to African Americans like Martin Luther King, Adam Clayton Powell, Paul Robeson, Harry T. Burleigh, and Ethel Waters. Carrie points out the Shearer Cottage, still in use as the first African American owned summer guest house allowed to receive visitors of color. A black woman, Mrs. Smith, once bought an Oak Bluffs Camp Ground cottage from her former employer to take in guests but a "liberal- acting" selectman named Mathews "settled" her in a suitable house he found for her elsewhere. Mrs. Tankard also shows me where Dorothy West, novelist from Harlem, lived for many years in the summer and "wrote and wrote and wrote." Her former companion-housekeeper now owns the cottage. Rev. Powell's cottage sits just down the street.

Carrie sends me on my way to make a last stop on the trail, the Eastville Graveyard, burial place for a few seafarers and others apparently "unwanted in the towns'" cemeteries. Here, the second Rebecca is thought to rest. Just past the Oak Bluffs Lobster Hatchery's parking lot, behind a nest of huge chemical tanks and a discarded underwater cage big enough for a lion lies a plot grown up with cedars and untamed shrubbery which almost hide the half dozen stones in the place. A pile of building material and assorted rubbish occupy one side of the yard. Some of the stones bear readable names: Alonzo E. Huston, 1882; Our Beloved Brother Samuel McLoud who died aboard the schooner A.V. Wellington, December 22, 1877; Mr. John Gates of Portsmouth, N. H., who died at sea April 30th, 1828; Samuel Lockwood who deceased this life October the 28th, 1801. The stone on a newly placed granite bench facing the others reads, "Nobody knows the trouble I've seen. - Rebecca Michael 1809 - 1854".

As I drive home I remember that another site of the Heritage Trail lies closer to home - a pair of stained glass windows at Grace Church, Vineyard Haven, honoring The Reverend Absolom Jones, first ordained African-American Episcopal Priest and The Right Reverend John Burgess, first African-American Episcopal Diocesan Bishop. I say hello to John Burgess in person almost every Sunday after church.

Everyone will travel the Heritage Trail with different memories and different perceptions. I've experienced the richness of inclusion and diversity but not without remnants of the opposite, not only from the past but in the here and now.

HOW TO GET THERE: I would recommend strongly obtaining Weintraub and Tankard's book, "African American Heritage Trail of Martha's Vineyard" or back copies of "Vineyard Style," Fall and Holiday Editions, 2000, for the entire list of sites and their locations.

[I am indebted to both Ms. Eileen Cawley Weintraub and Ms. Carrie Camillo Tankard for their generosity in time spent talking with me in preparation for this article.]

Lilly   the Author

Epilogue

Last Walk

She stretches full-length in front of the Vermont Castings wood stove on a chill February evening. Her lower cud on the downside of her mouth flops open showing perfect enamel for her age. Her flanks rise and fall in quiet breathing except for the liquid trill emanating from her short thick neck – the snore she has had since first arriving at eight weeks of age twelve years ago. Lilly's been with us a lifetime it seems. Her predecessor, Freckles, almost a twin, had shared our lives for the twelve years before the new arrival. Together, for most of our senior years (from our 50's and halfway through our 70's), these two springer spaniels have been our constant companions.

The next morning I walk up our field to where Freckles lies. Her now unmarked grave has mysteriously disappeared beneath a row of bountiful autumn olives and Rosa ragosa which grow everywhere around our place unless we mow them down. Lilly follows my path from the back steps. She tilts her head to one side as if to say, "What's so interesting up here at this time of year?" Her weather-stained tennis ball lies against the garden fence and I give it a toss toward the house. In a dash, reminiscent of her youth, she hustles the ball but immediately captures her ancient plaything and hides it from view under her crossed front legs. "No repeats today, thank-you," she says. In fact, while I reconnoiter around the other side of the yard she retreats to the back porch and dismembers the ball once and for all.

LET'S WALK, LILLY

"C'mon, Lill," I call. "Let's walk." If I slip the leash over her head she'll rise to her feet. I can tell from recent weeks she no longer follows me anywhere I lead. "No, not that way," she'll say. "That's up-hill. Down here to the beach and that ripe sea-gull to roll in." The last is left unsaid, just assumed by her knowing companion. Words aren't necessary to tell me I'm losing an argument, just the force of her dug-in front paws and the tilt of her head down-hill. I follow – her slave. At pond-edge with wind flattening her ears against the sides of her head, she stands directly at the source as if savoring the wind song of memory and surveying her domain. After a bit she relents to my gentle tugging and follows along the beach with interminable pauses and sniffing. She noses under the dry eel grass along the edge of the inland marsh, moving ever so steadily toward her favorite dead raccoon. In some strange act of nature this poor animal has floated among the detritus of the marsh for months without falling victim to the scavenging gulls, turkey vultures or the rare eagle. More to the point, I have kept Lilly from her mandatory roll in such an inviting carcass, one of my few victories over her canine instincts.

On the way up from the beach, Lilly begins to limp. Both left legs appear to be lame, a familiar observation in past weeks after walking a little too far from home. She seems in no rush to go anywhere until the back steps are in view. Then, free of her leash, she makes straightway for the house where she noses at the back door for the warmth she knows lies within.

"Oh, Lilly, how do we know when it is your time to leave us? You seem not to be going off under your own power. A short walk like this makes you limp and not want to go the next time. I understand. You've grown deaf so you no longer hear our calls. Your sight is barely enough to distinguish a figure at the top of the drive. You bark at me as you would a stranger bent on forcing an entry – until, that is, when I come close enough for you to smell. Then it's the old bark and wagging and attempts at jumping until we have to kneel down and give you dozens of rubs and scratches until you finally retire under the table to your bed. I can't forget to give your insulin today. It's more than you've ever had to take before. Please don't get me up too many times during the night to go outside and pee."

Lilly died a month after this last walk and lies now near her two old friends, Freckles and the cat, Kimba.

This piece was written for
The Martha's Vineyard Times edition of May 30, 2002.

Vineyard Walking Trails

Not all trails are covered in this book.

Land Bank

AQUINNAH

Moshup Beach —4.7 acres

Moshup Beach Overlook – 6.1 acres

CHILMARK

Fulling Mill Brook Preserve – 49.6 acres

Allen Farm – 22.5 acres

Peaked Hill Reservation – 93.4 acres

Chilmark Pond Preserve – 8.3 acres

Great Rock Bight – 28.5 acres

Waskosim's Rock Reservation – 184.9 acres

Middle Ridge Preserve – 7 acres

WEST TISBURY

Christiantown Woods – 8.6 acres

Wompesket Preserve – 18.1 acres

Priester's Pond Preserve – 2.9 acres

Sepiessa Point Reservation – 164.4 acres

Old County Arboretum – 2.5 acres

Child Farm – 17.5 acres

Duarte's Pond – 18.8 acres

TISBURY

Tisbury Meadow – 83.3 acres

Ripley's Field Preserve – 56.1 acres

Wilfrid's Pond Preserve – 3.2 acres

Ramble Trail Preserve – 7.3 acres

OAK BLUFFS
- Farm Pond Preserve – 27.2 acres
- Trade Wind Fields – 71.8 acres
- Wapatequa Woods – 19.6 acres
- Quay's Corner – 0.6 acres
- Pecoy Point Preserve – 14.3 acres
- Featherstone Farm – 18 acres

EDGARTOWN
- Katama Point Preserve – 2.1 acres
- Muskoday Farm – 28 acres
- Norton Fields Preserve – 15.5 acres

CHAPPAQUIDDICK
- Brine's Pond Preserve – 44 acres
- Chappy Five Corners – 45 acres
- Poucha Pond Reservation – 146.8 acres
- Chappy Point Beach – 2.9 acres
- N. Neck Highlands Preserve – 4.6 acres

Sheriff's Meadow Foundation

CHILMARK
- Middle Road Sanctuary – 110 acres
- Roth Woodlands – 26 acres

WEST TISBURY
- Cedar Tree Neck Sanctuary – 312 acres
- Nat's Farm Meadow – 55 acres

TISBURY
- West Chop Woods – 85 acres
- Brightwood Park – 9 acres

EDGARTOWN
- Sheriff's Meadow Sanctuary – 17 acres
- Caroline Tuthill Preserve – 154 acres

Mass. Audubon Society

EDGARTOWN
Felix Neck Wildlife Sanctuary – 350 acres

Trustees of Reservations

CHILMARK
Menemsha Hills – 211 acres

WEST TISBURY
Long Point Wildlife Refuge – 633 acres

CHAPPAQUIDDICK
Cape Pogue Wildlife Refuge – 516 acres

Mytoi – 14 acres

Wasque Reservation – 200 acres

Land Trusts on Martha's Vineyard

The Martha's Vineyard Land Bank Commission
PO Box 2057 • Edgartown, MA 02539
508-627-7141 • E-mail: mvlbc@capecod.net

The Sheriff's Meadow Foundation
RR1 Box 319X • Vineyard Haven, MA 02568
508-693-5207 • Web: www.sheriffsmeadow.org

The Massachusetts Audubon Society
PO Box 494 • Vineyard Haven, MA 02568
508-627-4850 • E-mail: felixneck@massaudubon.org

The Trustees of Reservations
PO Box 2106 • Vineyard Haven, MA 02568
508-693-7662 • Web: www.thetrustees.org.

photo by J.J. Gonson

The Author
Russell Hoxsie, MD

Russ Hoxsie, grew up in southeastern Massachusetts, was educated in Dartmouth and Wellesley schools, received his BA at Wesleyan University and his MD from Cornell Medical College. He retired in 1997, after 42 years of family medicine practice on the island of Martha's Vineyard. He has written articles on public health, especially tick related diseases and occasional book reviews. He has published a few of his own poems. He hopes to find a publisher for his memoir recounting the mental illness of one of his daughters and continues writing a bi-monthly column, "Off North Road," for The Martha's Vineyard Times. His other pastimes are gardening, walking, reading and enjoying his springer spaniel. He lives with his wife, Mary Ann, overlooking Menemsha Pond on the Vineyard. They have four grown children and six grandchildren.